New Collection 20

중학교 영어로 다시 읽는 세계명작

크리스마스 캐럴

A Christmas Carol

Charles Dickens 원작

넥서스콘텐츠개발팀 엮음

넥서스

중학교 영어로 다시 읽는 세계명작
New Collection 20
크리스마스 캐럴

원 작 Charles Dickens
엮은이 넥서스콘텐츠개발팀
펴낸이 안용백
펴낸곳 (주)넥서스

초판 1쇄 인쇄 2012년 9월 25일
초판 1쇄 발행 2012년 9월 30일

출판신고 1992년 4월 3일 제311-2002-2호
121-840 서울시 마포구 서교동 394-2
Tel (02)330-5500 Fax (02)330-5555

ISBN 978-89-5994-427-9 14740
ISBN 978-89-5797-467-4 14740 (세트)

가격은 뒤표지에 있습니다.
잘못 만들어진 책은 구입처에서 바꾸어 드립니다.

www.nexusbook.com

머 리 말

어릴 적 즐겨 읽었던 『이상한 나라의 앨리스』나 『작은 아씨들』을 이제 영어로 만나 보세요. 지난날 우리들을 설레게 했던 명작들을 영어로 읽어봄으로써, 우리말로는 느끼지 못했던 또 다른 재미와 감동을 느낄 수 있습니다. 또한 친숙한 이야기를 영어로 바꿔 읽는 것은 그 어느 학습 자료보다도 효과적입니다. 자신이 알고 있는 이야기를 떠올리며 앞으로 전개될 내용을 상상하며 읽어 나가면, 낯선 내용을 읽을 때만큼 어렵거나 부담스럽지 않기 때문입니다.

『중학교 · 고등학교 영어로 다시 읽는 세계명작 시리즈 New Collection』은 기존에 나와 있는 명작 시리즈와는 달리, 소설책을 읽듯 추억과 감동에 빠져들 수 있도록 원서의 느낌을 최대한 살렸습니다. 또한, 영한 대역 스타일을 탈피하여 우리말 번역을 권말에 배치함으로써 독자 여러분이 스스로 이야기를 이해하는 연습을 할 수 있도록 하였습니다. 더불어 원어민 성우들이 정확한 발음과 풍부한 감성으로 녹음한 MP3 파일은 눈과 귀로 벅찬 감동을 동시에 경험하며, 최대의 학습 효과를 얻을 수 있도록 제작되었습니다.

'순수하고 가슴 뭉클한 그 무엇'이 절실한 요즘, 주옥같은 세계명작을 다시금 읽으며 잠시나마 마음의 여유를 갖고 영어소설이 주는 감동에 빠져 보세요.

넥서스콘텐츠개발팀

이 시리즈의 특징

1 읽기 쉬운 영어로 Rewriting

한국인이 가장 좋아하는 세계명작만을 엄선하여, 원문을 최대한 살리면서 중고등학교 수준의 쉬운 영어로 각색하였다. 『중학교 영어로 다시 읽는 세계명작 시리즈 New Collection』은 1,000단어, 『고등학교 영어로 다시 읽는 세계명작 시리즈 New Collection』은 2,000단어 수준으로 각색하고, 어려운 어휘는 별도로 설명하여 사전 없이도 읽을 수 있다.

2 학습 효과를 배가시키는 Summary

각 STORY 및 SCENE이 시작될 때마다 우리말 요약을 제시하여 내용을 추측하면서 읽을 수 있기 때문에, 원서의 부담을 덜면서 더 큰 학습 효과를 얻을 수 있다.

3 학습용 MP3 파일

전문 원어민 성우들의 실감나는 연기가 담긴 MP3 파일을 들으면서, 읽기와 함께 듣기 및 말하기까지 연습할 수 있다.

4 독자를 고려한 최적의 디자인

한 손에 쏙 들어오는 판형, 읽기 편한 서체와 크기 등 독자가 언제 어디서나 오랜 시간 즐겁게 읽을 수 있도록 최상의 편집 체제와 세련된 디자인으로 가독성을 높였다.

추 천 리 딩 가 이 드

step 1 **청해** 들으면서 의미 추측하기

책을 읽기에 앞서 MP3 파일을 들으며 이야기의 내용을 추측해 본다.

step 2 **속독** 빨리 읽으면서 의미 추측하기

STORY 및 SCENE의 영문 제목과 우리말 요약을 읽은 다음, 본문을 읽으면서 혼자 힘으로 뜻을 파악해 본다. 모르는 단어나 문장이 나와도 멈추지 말고 전체적인 흐름을 파악하는 데 주력한다.

step 3 **정독** 정확히 읽으면서 의미 파악하기

어구 풀이와 권말 번역을 참고하면서 정확한 의미를 파악한다.

step 4 **낭독** 소리 내어 읽으면서 소리와 친해지기

단어와 단어가 연결될 때 나타나는 발음 현상과 속도 등에 유의하면서 큰 소리로 또박또박 읽어 본다.

step 5 **섀도잉** 따라 말하면서 회화 연습하기

MP3 파일을 들으며 원어민의 말을 한 박자 늦게 돌림노래 부르듯 따라 말하면서, 속도감과 발음 등 회화에 효과적인 훈련을 한다.

이 시리즈의 구성

우리말 Summary

이야기를 읽기 전에 내용을 짐작해 봄으로써, 편안한 마음으로 읽을 수 있도록 우리말 요약문을 제시하였다. 이를 힌트 삼아 보다 효과적인 내용 이해가 가능할 것이다.

영문

부담스러워 보이지 않고 편안하게 술술 읽히도록 서체와 크기, 간격 등을 최적의 체제로 편집하였다.

어구 풀이

이야기를 이해하는 데 도움이 되도록 어려운 어구를 순서대로 정리하였다. 이야기에 사용되는 의미를 우선순위로 하였으나, 2차적 의미가 중요하거나 불규칙 활용을 하는 경우도 함께 다뤄주어, 보다 풍부한 어구 학습이 되도록 배려하였다.

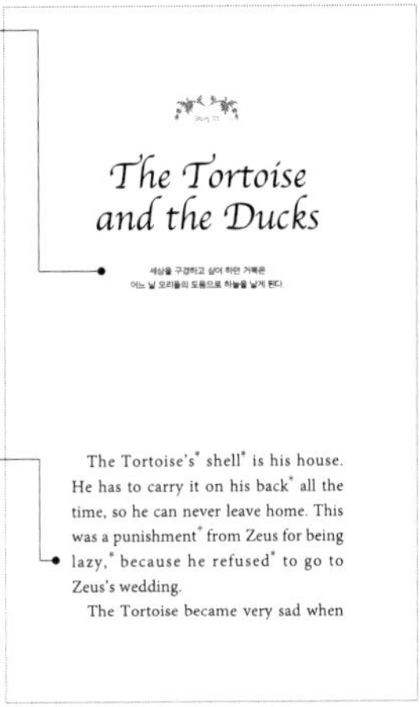

The Tortoise and the Ducks

세상을 구경하고 싶어 하던 거북은 어느 날 오리들의 도움으로 하늘을 날게 된다.

The Tortoise's* shell* is his house. He has to carry it on his back* all the time, so he can never leave home. This was a punishment* from Zeus for being lazy,* because he refused* to go to Zeus's wedding.

The Tortoise became very sad when

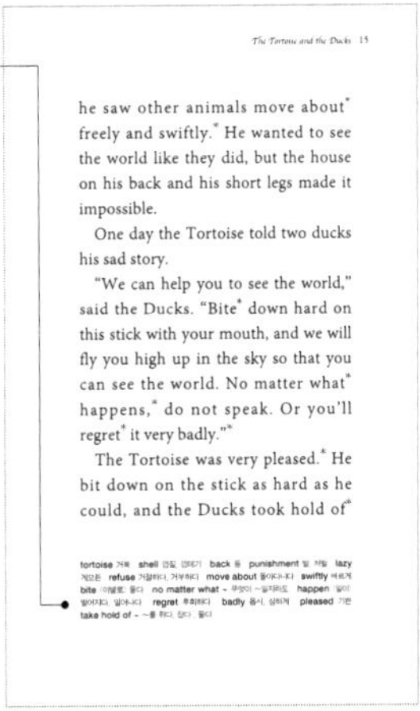

The Tortoise and the Ducks 15

he saw other animals move about* freely and swiftly.* He wanted to see the world like they did, but the house on his back and his short legs made it impossible.

One day the Tortoise told two ducks his sad story.

"We can help you to see the world," said the Ducks. "Bite* down hard on this stick with your mouth, and we will fly you high up in the sky so that you can see the world. No matter what* happens,* do not speak. Or you'll regret* it very badly."*

The Tortoise was very pleased.* He bit down on the stick as hard as he could, and the Ducks took hold of*

tortoise 거북 shell 껍질, 껍데기 back 등 punishment 벌, 처벌 lazy 게으른 refuse 거절하다, 거부하다 move about 돌아다니다 swiftly 빠르게 bite (이빨로) 물다 no matter what ~ 무엇이 ~일지라도 happen (일이) 벌어지다, 일어나다 regret 후회하다 badly 몹시, 심하게 pleased 기쁜 take hold of ~ ~를 쥐다, 잡다, 물다

우리말 번역

문장 구성과 어구의 쓰임을 효율적으로 학습할 수 있도록 직역을 기본으로 하여 번역하였다. 가능하면 번역에 의존하지 말고 영문과 어구만으로 이야기를 이해하도록 하며, 번역은 참고만 하도록 한다.

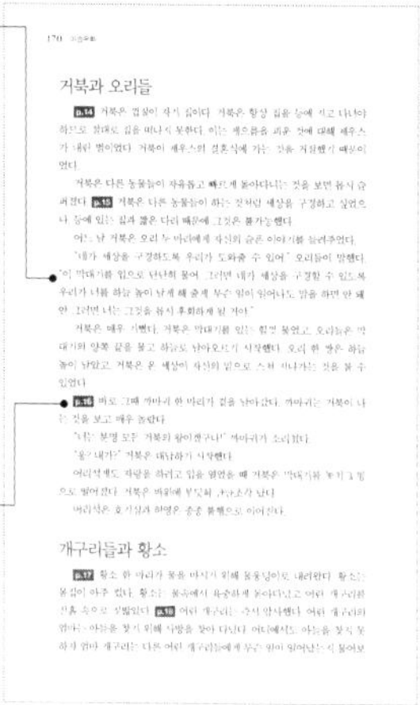

페이지 표시

영문을 읽다가 해결되지 않는 부분이 있을 때 그에 대응하는 번역 부분을 손쉽게 찾을 수 있도록 해당 영문 페이지의 번호를 표시해 놓았다.

MP3 파일
www.nexusbook.com에서 다운로드

전문 원어민 성우들의 생생한 연기를 귀로 들으며, 바로 옆에서 누군가가 동화책을 읽어주는 것처럼 더욱 흥미롭고 효과적으로 학습할 수 있다.

저자 소개

찰스 디킨즈(Charles Dickens, 1812~1870)는 영국 포츠머스에서 하급 해군 관리였던 존 디킨즈의 8남매 중 차남으로 태어났다. 하지만 그는 불우한 가정환경으로 인해 학교에 가는 대신 열두 살 때부터 돈을 벌기 위해 런던의 한 구두약 공장에서 하루에 10시간씩 일해야 했다. 이때의 경험은 훗날 그의 자전적인 소설인 「데이비드 코퍼필드」에 그대로 투영되는데, 어린 나이에 열악한 환경에서 노동자의 신분으로 얼마나 큰 고통과 좌절을 겪고 그것이 훗날까지 상처로 남은 경위를 잘 보여 준다.

이후 중등 교육을 2년 정도 받고 변호사 사무실에서 사환으로 일하다가 법원의 속기사를 거쳐 신문사의 속기 기자가 되었다. 어린 시절 틈틈이 읽어 두었던 고전에 대한 지식과 기자 생활로 얻은 풍부한 경험과 식견은 그의 작품 활동에 큰 영향을 미쳤다. 1833년에 본격적으로 작가의 길로 들어선 찰스는 1836년에 단편집 「보즈의 스케치」를 출간했고 이어서 발표한 「올리버 트위스트」가 문학성과 상업성 면에서 동시에 성공을 거두며 유명 작가가 되었다. 이후 그는 「위대한 유산」, 「두 도시 이야기」, 「크리스마스 캐럴」 등과 같은 수작들을 잇달아 집필했다. 이러한 공로로 1870년에는 빅토리아 여왕으로부터 기사 작위를 수여받았으나, 귀족의 신분을 거부하고 평민으로 남았다. 그는 1870년 「에드윈 드루드의 수수께끼」를 집필하던 중 과로로 사망했고 웨스트민스터 대성당에 안장되었다.

작품 소개

천하의 구두쇠이자 지독한 수전노인 스크루지에게는 모두가 즐거워하는 일 년에 단 하루뿐인 크리스마스도 아무 의미가 없다. 단지 이날 일하지도 않는 직원에게 급료를 주는 것이 아까울 뿐이다. 그는 불쌍한 사람들을 위해 기부금을 받으러 온 사람들을 매정하게 내쫓고, 저녁 식사 초대를 하러 온 조카에게도 박정하게 군다. 그런 스크루지 영감에게 죽은 동업자 말리의 유령이 찾아와 자신의 비참한 모습을 보여 주며 그의 삶의 방식에 대해 경고한다. 이후 차례로 찾아온 크리스마스 유령들은 스크루지의 과거, 현재, 미래의 모습을 보여 주고, 그는 이를 통해 깨달음을 얻어 모두에게 존경 받는 삶을 살게 된다.

스크루지는 이 작품의 저자인 찰스 디킨즈가 살았던 19세기 중반, 산업혁명 이후 급속히 대두된 자본주의와 이로 인해 발생한 사회적 모순을 상징하는 인물이다. 디킨즈는 이 작품을 통해 자본주의의 이면인 탐욕과 빈익빈 부익부 현상을 교묘하게 꼬집으며 착취당하고 억압받는 사람들에게 필요한 사회적 배려와 관심을 촉구하고 있다. 전형적인 권선징악적 줄거리 구조이지만 신비로운 유령을 등장시키고 시공을 넘나드는 환상적인 배경을 더하여 작품에 신선함을 주고 이야기를 독특하게 연출하는 데 성공했다. 이 작품은 대중의 많은 사랑을 받았고, 아직까지도 크리스마스를 소재로 한 작품 가운데 가장 유명한 작품이자 불멸의 고전으로 남아 있다.

Contents

Chapter 01

Marley's Ghost

스크루지는 지독한 구두쇠 영감이다.
어느 크리스마스이브에 잠이 든 스크루지에게
고인이 된 말리의 유령이 찾아와 스크루지의 삶의 방식에 대해 경고한다.

Marley was dead. There is no doubt about that. The clergyman,* the clerk,* and the undertaker* all signed a paper that said he was dead. Scrooge also signed it. And Scrooge never signed something that wasn't true. Old Marley was as dead as a doornail.*

Did Scrooge know he was dead? Of course he did. How could he not know? Scrooge and he were partners* for many years. Scrooge was his only lawyer,* his only coworker,* his only friend, and the only guest at his funeral.* But even Scrooge was not very sad that he had died. He was a true businessman* and made sure that he got a good bargain* for the price of the funeral.

Anyway, there must be no doubt in your mind that Marley was dead. If you do not really believe that he is dead, the story I will tell you will be less wonderful. If you do not believe that someone is dead, is seeing him stroll* outside at night still amazing? If you heard his voice whispering in the wind, would you still be

clergyman 목사, 성직자 **clerk** 서기 **undertaker** 장의사 **as dead as a doornail** 완전히 죽은 **partner** 동료, 협력자 **lawyer** 법률가, 변호사 **coworker** 동료 **funeral** 장례식 **businessman** 사업가 **good bargain** 싼 물건, 싼 거래 **stroll** 한가로이 거닐다

frightened*?

Both Scrooge and Marley's names were still painted on the door of their office building. Scrooge had never erased* it. The company was known as Scrooge and Marley's. Sometimes new customers called Scrooge by his real name, and sometimes they called him Marley. He answered to both names. It was all the same to him.

Oh! But he was a mean,* greedy,* old SCROOGE*! His heart was as hard as steel.* There was a coldness inside him that froze* the tip* of his nose and his cheeks. It made him walk as straight* as a board.* It made his eyes red and his thin lips blue. It even made his voice sound scratchy* and cold. He always carried his own low temperature* with him. He made his office cold even on the hottest days of summer, and he never became warm, even at Christmas.

No warmth* could warm him, and no wintry* weather could chill* him. No wind that blew was bitterer* than he was. No falling snow or rain was as determined* as he was. The heaviest rain or snow only did one thing better than Scrooge. Sometimes falling snow or rain looks quite pretty. Scrooge never looked pretty.

Nobody ever stopped him in the street to greet* him. No beggars* asked him for money, no children asked him about the time, no man or woman ever asked him for directions. Even the blind men's dogs seemed to know him. When they saw him coming, they would pull their owners away from him. They were scared of his evil* eye!

---

frightened 깜짝 놀란, 겁이 난 **erase** 지우다 **mean** 인색한, 쩨쩨한 **greedy** 탐욕스러운 **scrooge** 구두쇠, 수전노 **steel** 강철 **freeze** 얼다, 얼어붙다 **tip** 끝, 끄트머리 **straight** 곧은, 일직선의 **board** 판자 **scratchy** 긁히는 소리가 나는 **temperature** 온도 **warmth** 온기 **wintry** 차가운, 냉랭한 **chill** 춥게 하다; 냉기, 한기 **bitter** 지독한, 가혹한 **determined** 결연한, 단호한 **greet** ~에게 인사하다 **beggar** 거지 **evil** 사악한, 부도덕한

But Scrooge didn't care! He liked it! He loved to walk through crowds of* people and watch them all become afraid of him. He loved to be alone.

One Christmas Eve, old Scrooge was busy counting his money. It was cold, gray and dangerous weather. The fog was so thick that it was hard to see. He could hear the people outside stomping their feet* loudly so that other people could know they were there. It was only three in the afternoon, but it was already dark. The weak light of candles* shone from the windows of the offices.

The fog came pouring in* through every crack* and keyhole.* It was so dense* that the other houses looked like ghosts. Seeing a cloud so thick hanging* over the city made people feel that nature was planning something strange. The door of Scrooge's office was open, so he could watch his clerk, who in a tiny, sad room was copying* letters. Scrooge had a very small fire, but the clerk's fire was so much smaller that it was only burning one piece of coal.*

He could not get more coal because Scrooge kept the coal in his office. If he asked for more, he was afraid that Scrooge would fire* him. The clerk wrapped* himself in his white blanket* and tried to warm* his hands with the candle. He still felt cold.

"A merry Christmas, Uncle!" cried a cheerful* voice. "God save you!"

It was the voice of Scrooge's nephew, who surprised him suddenly.

"Bah*!" said Scrooge. "Humbug*!"

crowds of 많은 **stomp one's feet** 발을 세게 구르다, 육중하게 걷다 **candle** 양초 **pour in** 쏟아져 들어오다 **crack** 갈라진 금, 틈 **keyhole** 열쇠 구멍 **dense** 자욱한, 짙은 **hang** 걸다, 달아매다 **copy** 베끼다, 복사하다 **coal** 석탄 **fire** 해고하다 **wrap** 감싸다 **blanket** 담요, 모포 **warm** 따뜻하게 하다, 데우다 **cheerful** 명랑한, 유쾌한 **bah** 흥, 체 **humbug** 허튼소리

Scrooge's nephew had walked so quickly in the fog that he felt he was warm. His face was red and handsome. His eyes sparkled,* and his breath* smoked.*

"Christmas is a humbug, Uncle?" said Scrooge's nephew. "You don't mean that, I am sure?"

"I do," said Scrooge. "A merry Christmas? Why would you be merry? What reason do you have to be merry? You're poor."

"Well, why are you unhappy?" said the nephew. "What reason do you have to be angry? You're rich."

"Bah! Humbug," he said again.

"Don't be angry, Uncle!" said the nephew.

"What else can I be when I live in a world of fools?" grumbled* Scrooge. "A merry Christmas? Who cares about Christmas! Christmas is a time for paying bills* when you have no money! You are a year older but not any richer! You can think about how twelve months have disappeared*! If I could, I would boil* everyone who says a merry Christmas!"

"Uncle!" begged the nephew.

"Nephew, you keep Christmas in your way," said Scrooge, "and let me keep it in mine."

"I can't hear you say these things at Christmas," said the nephew.

"Leave me alone, then! What will you get if you change my mind? Do you think I will give you a present?" said Scrooge.

"Just because I don't get something doesn't mean I get nothing good," said the nephew. "I don't care what others think about Christmas, but for me it's

sparkle 빛나다 **breath** 숨, 입김 **smoke** 연기가 나다, 김이 오르다 **grumble** 투덜거리다, 불평하다 **bill** 청구서, 계산서 **disappear** 사라지다, 안 보이게 되다 **boil** 끓이다, 삶다

important. Of course I care about* Christmas as a holy* day. Yet it is also a day for sharing love with my family and friends. Even though Christmas has never given me gold or silver, it has still given me good things."

The clerk suddenly started clapping.* Then he realized* that his boss would be angry and stopped. He shyly* began to poke* the small fire.

"If you make another noise, clerk, I'll fire you!" said Scrooge. "You're quite a powerful* speaker, sir," he added,* turning to his nephew. "Why don't you go into politics*?"

"Don't be angry, Uncle," said the nephew. "Come! Have dinner with us tomorrow."

"I would rather eat by myself than have dinner with your family," said Scrooge.

"But why?" cried Scrooge's nephew.

"Why?"

"Why did you get married?" asked Scrooge.

"Because I fell in love," replied the nephew.

"Because you fell in love!" growled* Scrooge, as if that were the only one thing in the world more ridiculous* than a merry Christmas. "Good afternoon!"

"You just don't want to see us because we are in love?" said the nephew. "That's not a good reason!"

"Good afternoon," said Scrooge.

"I want nothing from you," said the nephew. "I ask nothing of you. Why can't we be friends?"

"Good afternoon," said Scrooge.

"I am sorry, with all my heart,* to find you so determined," said the nephew. "I

---

care about ~에 마음 쓰다, 관심을 가지다 **holy** 거룩한, 신성한 **clap** 박수를 치다 **realize** 깨닫다 **shyly** 소심하게, 멋쩍게 **poke** 찌르다, 쑤시다 **powerful** 힘 있는, 강력한 **add** 덧붙이다 **go into politics** 정치에 입문하다 **growl** 으르렁거리다 **ridiculous** 웃기는, 우스꽝스러운 **with all one's heart** 진심으로

didn't mean to make you angry. I can't understand you, but I still want you to have a good Christmas. So a merry Christmas, Uncle!"

"Good afternoon!" said Scrooge.

"And a happy New Year!" said the nephew.

"Good afternoon!" said Scrooge.

His nephew left the office without an angry word. He stopped at the door to wish the clerk a merry Christmas, who, cold as he was, still returned the greetings warmly.

"There's another fool," grumbled Scrooge who heard him. "My clerk, with his small salary, and a wife and family, is talking about a merry Christmas."

This crazy fool, as he let the nephew out, let two people inside. They were fat gentlemen who looked pleasant. They stood, with their hats off, in Scrooge's office. They had books and papers in their hands and bowed* to him.

"Is this Scrooge and Marley's?" said one of the gentlemen, looking at his list.* "Do I have the pleasure of meeting Mr. Scrooge or Mr. Marley?"

"Mr. Marley has been dead for seven years," replied Scrooge. "He died seven years ago, this very night."

"We have no doubt that you, his partner, would do what he wanted you to do," said the gentleman, who showed his credentials.*

In fact, Scrooge and Marley had been very similar.* Scrooge looked at the credentials and then back at the gentleman.

"Because it is Christmas time, Mr. Scrooge," said one of the gentlemen,

---

bow 머리를 숙이다, 절하다 **list** 목록 **credentials** 자격 증명서, 신분증명서
similar 비슷한, 유사한

"it is more important than usual that we give something to the poor. They suffer* greatly at the present time.* Many thousands do not have basic* things, like food, water, or shelter.* Many hundreds are in need of* comfort.*"

"Are there no prisons?" asked Scrooge.

"There are many prisons," said the gentleman as he put down his pen.

"And the workhouses*?" added Scrooge. "Are they still working?"

"They are," said the gentleman. "I wish I could say they were not."

"Are there many poor people in the workhouses or locked in prisons?" asked Scrooge.

"Yes, very many," replied the gentleman.

"Oh!" said Scrooge. "I was afraid, from what you said at first, that something had changed. I'm very glad to hear it."

"The poor have no Christmas spirit* or

cheer,*" said the gentleman. "A few of us are trying to raise money* to buy the poor some meat, drinks, and warm blankets and clothes. We choose this time because it is a time, of all others,* when poor people really want things for everyday life. What do you wish to give?"

"Nothing!" Scrooge replied.

"We don't have to write down your name," said the gentleman. "If you don't want other people to know that you gave us money, you can give anonymously.*"

"I wish to be left alone," said Scrooge. "Since you ask me what I wish, gentlemen, that is my answer. I don't have merry Christmases, and I don't want to make other people feel merry at Christmas. I help to support* the prisons and the

suffer 고통을 겪다 **at the present time** 현재 **basic** 기본적인 **shelter** 주거, 집 **in need of** ~을 필요로 하는 **comfort** 위로, 위안 **workhouse** 구빈원 **spirit** 정신; 혼령, 유령 **cheer** 기분, 원기 **raise money** 모금하다 **of all others** 모든 것 중에서 **anonymously** 익명으로 **support** 후원하다

workhouses. The poor can go there!"

"Not many can go there," said the gentleman. "And many people say they would rather die than go there."

"If they would rather die, then they should die," said Scrooge. "That way, we can decrease* the population.* There are already too many people in this country."

"We must all help the poor," said the gentleman.

"It's not my business," said Scrooge. "I take care of myself. I am always busy helping myself. Good afternoon, gentlemen!"

Seeing clearly that it would be useless* to keep asking, the gentlemen left Scrooge's office. Scrooge continued* working with an improved* opinion* of himself.

Meanwhile,* the fog and darkness thickened* so much that people ran around the streets with lanterns. The ancient* church tower that always secretly watched Scrooge through his window was now invisible.* High up in the clouds, its bell rang. Its voice shook as if it had teeth that were shivering* in the cold. The cold became stronger.

In the main street, at the corner of the town square,* some workers were repairing* the gas pipes. They had lit a great fire, and around it, a party* of poor men and boys were gathered.* They gladly warmed their hands there. The water on the street had suddenly turned to ice. The bright light from the shops made the men's pale* faces look reddish.*

Butcher's shops* and grocery stores* began to have fun, selling their products.

decrease 줄이다 **population** 인구, 주민 수 **useless** 무익한, 소용없는 **continue** 계속하다 **improved** 향상된 **opinion** 평가, 의견 **meanwhile** 한편, 그사이 **thicken** 짙어지다 **ancient** 오래된 **invisible** 눈에 보이지 않는 **shiver** 떨리다, 추워로 떨다 **square** 광장 **repair** 수선하다, 수리하다 **party** 일행, 일단 **gather** 모이다, 집결하다 **pale** 창백한 **reddish** 불그스름한, 불그레한 **butcher's shop** 정육점 **grocery store** 식품점

The Lord Mayor,* who lived in his great, big house, told his fifty chefs* and butlers* to go home to their families. Even the little tailor,* who usually made trouble* on the streets, was at home making Christmas pudding. Meanwhile, his wife and baby went to buy some meat.

It became still foggier and colder. It was a biting,* piercing* chill. If the wolves and bears still lived in London, even they would feel cold on this night. A small young man who was very hungry and bitterly* cold knocked on Scrooge's door. He wanted to sing a Christmas carol* to him.

"God bless* you, merry gentleman!" he sang to Scrooge as he opened the door. "May nothing bring you sadness!" Scrooge grabbed* his ruler so quickly that the small young man ran away in terror.*

Finally it was the time to close the office

and go home. Angrily, Scrooge got down from his stool* and told the clerk to go home. The clerk put his candle out* and put on his hat.

"You'll want to stay home with your family tomorrow?" said Scrooge.

"If I can, yes," said the clerk.

"I don't want you to," said Scrooge. "And it's not fair. If I didn't pay you when you worked, you would be angry?"

The clerk smiled faintly.*

"Yet, I'm supposed to* pay you for Christmas even though you don't work," said Scrooge.

"It is only once a year, sir," said the clerk.

"It's a poor excuse* for taking my money every twenty-fifth of December!" said

Lord Mayor 시장 **chef** 주방장 **butler** 집사, 하인 **tailor** 재단사, 재봉사 **make trouble** 소동을 일으키다 **biting** 살을 에는 듯한 **piercing** 찌르는 듯한 **bitterly** 몹시, 지독하게 **carol** 축가, 캐럴 **bless** 축복하다 **grab** 움켜잡다 **in terror** 깜짝 놀라서, 혼비백산하여 **stool** 의자(등받이, 손잡이가 없는 의자) **put out** (불을) 끄다 **faintly** 희미하게, 어렴풋이 **be supposed to** ~하기로 되어 있다 **excuse** 구실, 핑계

Scrooge, buttoning* his great coat. "But I suppose* you must take the whole day off. Be here earlier the next morning."

The clerk promised that he would, and Scrooge walked out with a growl. The office was closed quickly. The clerk, with his white blanket around his waist,* ran home through the streets. He got home to his family as quickly as possible.

Scrooge had his melancholy* dinner in his usual melancholy tavern.* After he read all the newspapers, and spent the rest of the evening looking at his bankbook,* he went home to bed. He lived in one of the rooms which had once belonged to his dead partner. They were a sad set of rooms. It was strange to have a house in this place, because it looked so different from the other buildings around it. It was old now, lonely, and dreadful,* for nobody lived in it but* Scrooge. The other rooms were all offices.

The yard was so dark that even Scrooge, who knew its every stone, used his hands to find his way. The fog and frost* hung around the black gate as if they were made by the black gate itself. At any rate,* there was nothing special about the knocker* on the door, except that it was very large.

In fact,* Scrooge had seen this knocker every morning and night that he lived in this house. Also, Scrooge had very little imagination* and never daydreamed.* Furthermore,* Scrooge had not thought about his partner, Marley, since his last mention of his seven years' dead partner that afternoon. How can any man explain what happened next? When Scrooge

button 단추를 채우다 **suppose** 생각하다 **waist** 허리 **melancholy** 우울한, 감성에 젖은 **tavern** 선술집 **bankbook** 예금 통장 **dreadful** 아주 불쾌한, 음침한 **but** ~을 제외하고 **frost** 서리 **at any rate** 아무튼, 어쨌든 **knocker** (문에 달린) 쇠고리 **in fact** 실제로, 사실 **imagination** 상상(력) **daydream** 백일몽을 꿈꾸다, 공상에 잠기다 **furthermore** 더욱이, 게다가

unlocked* the door, he saw Marley's face in the knocker.

It surely was Marley's face. It was not under a dark shadow like the other objects* in the yard were, but it had a faint* light around it, like a bad lobster* in the cellar.* It was not angry or dangerous, but looked at Scrooge as Marley had usually looked at him.

It wore ghostly* glasses on its ghostly forehead.* The hair was curiously* messy* as if it were blown by wind. Also, although the eyes were wide open, they did not move. That, and its ugly color, made it look horrible. It did not seem to want to be horrible,* but it just was. Scrooge stared at* this ghost, and it was a knocker again.

To say that he was not surprised, or that his heart wasn't beating quickly, would be untrue.* But he put his hand upon the key he had dropped, turned it in the lock, opened the door, and walked inside.

He did stop to think for a moment before he closed the door. Before he did, he looked carefully behind it first, as if he half expected to see Marley on the other side. But there was nothing on the back of the door, except the screws* and nuts* that held the knocker.

"Pooh, pooh*!" he said and closed the door with a bang.*

The sound of it closing was like thunder.* Every room above, and every bottle in the wine merchant*'s cellars below, seemed to shake a little. Scrooge was not a man to be frightened by noises. He locked the door, walked across the hall, and up the stairs, slowly. He held his

unlock 자물쇠를 열다 **object** 물건, 물체 **faint** 희미한, 가냘픈 **lobster** 바닷가재 **cellar** 지하실, 지하층 **ghostly** 유령 같은, 희미한 **forehead** 이마 **curiously** 이상하게도 **messy** 흐트러진, 산란한 **horrible** 무서운, 끔찍한 **stare at** ~을 응시하다, 빤히 보다 **untrue** 진실이 아닌, 허위의 **screw** 나사 **nut** 너트, 암나사 **pooh** 흥, 제기랄 **bang** 쾅 하는 소리 **thunder** 천둥 **merchant** 상인

candle as he went.

The staircase* was so wide that there would still be extra room. This is perhaps the reason why Scrooge thought he saw a train with a hearse* driving up the stairs past him in the dark. Even six street lamps would not have lit the stairs well, so Scrooge's tiny candle barely* lit the way.

But Scrooge didn't care about the darkness and continued to climb the stairs. He liked darkness because it was cheap. But before he shut* his heavy door, he walked through his rooms to see that everything was okay. His memory* of Marley's face encouraged* him to be careful.

The living room, bedroom, and lumber room* were all as they should be. Nobody was under the table, and nobody was under the sofa. A small fire was in the fireplace,* the spoon and pot were ready, and the little bowl of gruel* was on the desk. Nobody was under the bed, nobody was in the closet,* and nobody was in his bathrobe,* which was hanging up in a creepy* way against the wall. Everything was normal.

Quite satisfied, he closed his door, and locked himself in. He even locked the second lock, which was not what he usually did. Thus, feeling safer, he changed his clothes and ate his gruel in front of the fire.

It was a very small fire on this bitterly cold night. He had to sit very closely in order to feel warm. The fireplace was an old one built by some Dutch* merchant long ago. It was decorated with tiles that had pictures based on* some stories from

staircase 계단 **hearse** 영구차 **barely** 간신히 **shut** 닫다 **memory** 기억, 추억 **encourage** 촉진하다, 조장하다 **lumber room** 창고 **fireplace** 벽난로 **gruel** 오트밀 죽 **closet** 벽장, 광 **bathrobe** 목욕용 가운 **creepy** 소름이 끼치는 **Dutch** 네덜란드의 **based on** ~에 토대를 둔

the Bible. On them were Cains and Abels, Pharaoh's daughters, Queens of Sheba, and angels floating* through the air on clouds like feather beds. On them were also hundreds of pretty little pictures that he could think about.

Yet that face of Marley, seven years dead, was the only thing he could think about and the only thing his eyes seemed to see. If each smooth* tile had been blank,* he would have imagined a copy of old Marley's head on every one.

"Humbug!" said Scrooge, and he walked across the room.

After several turns, he sat down again. As he threw his head back in the chair, his gaze* happened to rest upon an old bell that hung in the room. This bell that hadn't been used in a long time suddenly began to ring. To his great astonishment,* this bell began to swing.* It swung so softly at first that it barely made a sound. But soon it rang out loudly, and so did every bell in the house.

This might have lasted* half a minute, or a minute, but it seemed an hour. The bells stopped as they had begun, together. Next he heard a clanking* noise from deep down below. It sounded as if some person were dragging* a heavy chain over the bottles in the wine-merchant's cellar. Scrooge then remembered to have heard about ghosts in haunted* houses. They were described as carrying chains.

The cellar door flew open* with a booming* sound, and then he heard the noise much louder on the floors below. Then it was coming up the stairs. Then it was coming straight toward his door.

float (공중에서) 떠다니다 **smooth** 매끄러운 **blank** 빈, 공백의 **gaze** 주시, 응시 **to one's astonishment** ~가 깜짝 놀라게도 **swing** 흔들리다 **last** 계속하다, 지속하다 **clanking** 철거덕거리는 **drag** 끌다 **haunted** 귀신이 나오는 **fly open** (문 등이) 활짝 열리다 **booming** 쿵 하고 울리는

"It's humbug still!" said Scrooge. "I won't believe it."

His face turned completely white when something flew through the door. As the ghost entered the room, the flame* jumped up and down.

"I know him!" the flame seemed to say. "It's Marley's Ghost!"

It was Marley's Ghost. The Ghost's face was exactly the same as Marley's. It had Marley's hair, his pants, his jacket, and his high boots. The chain it carried was wrapped around its waist. It was long and hung from its back like a tail. It was made of cash boxes,* keys, locks, paperwork,* and heavy purses* made of steel. You could see through its body. As Scrooge watched it, he could see both the buttons on the front and back of its jacket.

Scrooge had often heard that Marley had no guts,* but he did not believe this until now. No, nor did he believe it even now. Though he stared at the Ghost, and saw it standing in front of him, and even though he felt the chill of its dead cold eyes, he still did not believe it. He closed his eyes over and over again* and tried to wish the ghost away.

"How now!" said Scrooge, cold and mean as usual. "What do you want with me?"

"Much!" said Marley's voice, no doubt about it.

"Who are you?" asked Scrooge.

"Ask me who I was," replied Marley's voice.

"Who were you, then?" said Scrooge, raising his voice.* "You're strange, for a ghost."

But how would he know? This was the

flame 불꽃, 불길 **cash box** 금고 **paperwork** 서류 **purse** 지갑, 손가방
have no guts 속이 없다, 비어 있다 **over and over again** 여러 번 계속하여
raise one's voice 목소리를 높이다

first ghost he had ever met.

"In life* I was your partner, Jacob Marley," said the Ghost.

"Can you...can you sit down?" asked Scrooge, looking doubtfully* at it.

"I can," said the Ghost.

"Do it, then," said Scrooge.

Scrooge asked the question because he didn't know whether a ghost could actually sit down in a chair or not. He felt that if it were impossible, the Ghost would become embarrassed* and have to give a long explanation.* But the Ghost sat down on the opposite* side of the fireplace as if it were quite used to* it.

"You don't believe in me," said the Ghost.

"I don't," said Scrooge.

"But you can see, hear, and feel me?" said the Ghost. "Why don't you believe in me?"

"I don't know," said Scrooge.

"Why do you doubt your senses?" asked the Ghost.

"Because senses can lie to you," replied Scrooge. "A little stomachache* can make you see things that aren't there. You may be a spoiled* bit of beef, some bad mustard,* a crumb* of cheese, or a piece of rotten* potato. You're just something a man sees because of a fever*!"

Scrooge actually did not usually get stomachaches. The truth is that he tried to be smart.* He tried to think of excuses, so that he would not have to think about the Ghost. The Ghost made him feel a horrible chill deep in his bones.*

If he sat and stared at those eyes that didn't move for a moment, he thought he

in life 현세에서 **doubtfully** 의심스럽게 **embarrassed** 어리둥절한, 당혹한 **explanation** 설명 **opposite** 반대편의, 맞은편의 **be used to** ~에 익숙해지다 **stomachache** 복통 **spoiled** 상한 **mustard** 겨자 **crumb** 작은 조각, 부스러기 **rotten** 썩은 **fever** 열, 신열 **smart** 영리한 **bone** 뼈

would go crazy. There was something very awful,* too, about how the Ghost made its own cold air. The Ghost also seemed to have its own wind. Even though it was sitting still, its clothes still moved as though a wind from under its feet were blowing them.

"You see this toothpick*?" said Scrooge. He tried to get the Ghost not to look at him and look at something else instead.*

"I do," replied the Ghost.

"You are not looking at it," said Scrooge.

"But I see it, anyway," said the Ghost.

"Well! If I swallow* this, I might die," said Scrooge. "Then I will only have my own thoughts to bother* me instead of ghosts outside, like you. Humbug, I tell you! Humbug!"

At this, the Ghost cried frightfully* and shook its chain with such a loud, dreadful noise that Scrooge held on tight* to his chair. He had to stop himself from fainting. Then the Ghost began to take off his bandages* as though they were too hot to wear inside. Suddenly, its lower jaw* dropped down onto its chest*!

Scrooge fell upon his knees and held his hands in front of its face.

"Mercy*!" he said. "Dreadful Ghost, why do you trouble me?"

"Man of the worldly* mind!" replied the Ghost. "Do you believe in me or not?"

"I do," said Scrooge. "I must. But why do spirits walk the earth, and why do they come to me?"

"All men must walk with other men and travel far and wide. If a man does not walk, travel, and learn from other men during his life, he will have to do it after he

awful 무서운, 무시무시한 **toothpick** 이쑤시개 **instead** 그 대신에 **swallow** 삼키다 **bother** 괴롭히다 **frightfully** 무섭게, 무시무시하게 **hold on tight** 세게 잡다 **bandage** 붕대 **jaw** 턱 **chest** 가슴 **mercy** 자비 **worldly** 세속적인, 속된 마음의

dies. He must wander* through the world, sadly, and see all the things he cannot have now. He must see all the happiness he could have had but now cannot share.*"

Again the Ghost cried and shook its chain loudly with its shadowy* hands.

"You have a chain around your waist," said Scrooge, shaking. "Tell me why."

"I wear the chain I made in life," replied the Ghost. "I made it link by link and yard by yard. It was my choice to make this chain and my choice to wear it. Is its pattern* strange to you?"

Scrooge shook more and more.

"Or would you know the weight* and length* of the strong chain you carry?" said the Ghost. "My chain has not changed since I died seven years ago. Your chain is just the same, but even longer!"

Scrooge looked around himself and the floor. He expected to see a chain around his body or in the room somewhere, but he saw nothing.

"Jacob," he begged. "Old Jacob Marley, tell me more. Speak comfort to me, Jacob!"

"I have nothing to give," the Ghost replied. "It comes from other Spirits who have had happier lives than me. Nor can I tell you everything that I want to tell you. I may only tell you a few things. I cannot rest. I cannot stay. I cannot live anywhere. When I was alive, I never walked further than our home or our office. So now, I must journey* many far places without rest."

Whenever Scrooge started thinking about something, he put his hands in his pants' pockets. While still sitting on his knees, he thought very deeply about what the Ghost said.

---

wander 돌아다니다 **share** 함께 나누다, 함께하다 **shadowy** 그림자 같은 **pattern** 방식, 무늬 **weight** 무게 **length** 길이 **journey** 여행하다

"You must have been traveling very slowly," said Scrooge, sounding like a businessman. But his voice was more shy than usual.

"Slowly!" repeated* the Ghost.

"You have been dead for seven years," said Scrooge, "and you still haven't finished traveling!"

"The whole time, no rest, no peace. I am always tortured* with regret,*" said the Ghost.

"You travel fast?" asked Scrooge.

"On the wings of the wind," replied the Ghost.

"So then, you must have been to many places in seven years," said Scrooge.

The Ghost, on hearing this, cried and shook its chains very loudly. It was so loud that Scrooge wondered* if the police might come and arrest* it for making too much noise on this silent night.

"Oh, yes, I have traveled!" cried the Ghost. "I have traveled in chains the whole time. If only living men knew how long they have to wait to find peace after they die! There were so many chances that I missed! I wasted* so much of my short time alive! Yet that's the choice I made! And now I must suffer."

"But you were always a good man of business, Jacob," said Scrooge, who now began to wonder if he was just like Marley.

"Business!" cried the Ghost, shaking its hands again. "My business was for mankind.* Helping people, charity,* mercy, kindness and sympathy* was my business. The money I made for our company was just a tiny part of my real business!"

repeat 반복하다, 따라 말하다 **torture** 고문하다, 심하게 괴롭히다 **with regret** 후회하며 **wonder** ~이 아닐까 생각하다, 궁금해 하다 **arrest** 체포하다 **waste** 낭비하다, 허비하다 **mankind** 인류, 인간 **charity** 자선, 보시 **sympathy** 동정, 연민

The Ghost held up its chain in front of it, as if that were the cause* of all its pain* and regret. Then it flung* it heavily on the floor again.

"At this time of the year, I suffer most," said the Ghost. "Why did I walk through crowds of men and never look at their faces? Why did I never think to help people who needed help? Why did I ignore* the problems of other men?"

Scrooge was very upset* by the things the Ghost was saying. He felt his whole body shake and shiver. He could not look at the Ghost's face.

"Hear me!" cried the Ghost. "My time is nearly gone."

"I will," said Scrooge. "But don't be hard upon me! Don't hurt* me, Jacob! Please!"

"I cannot tell you why you see me tonight," said the Ghost. "Truthfully, I have sat next to you and watched you many times, but you could not see me then."

This thought did not make Scrooge happy. Scrooge shivered and wiped* sweat* from his forehead.

"Usually I don't enjoy being invisible," continued the Ghost. "That is a part of my punishment.* I am here tonight to warn* you. You still have a chance and hope of escaping* my fate.* Ebenezer, I am here to tell you about this chance and hope."

"You were always a good friend to me," said Scrooge. "Thank you!"

"You will be haunted* by Three Spirits," continued the Ghost.

Scrooge's face dropped, and he again could not look at the Ghost.

"Is that the chance and hope you

cause 원인 **pain** 아픔, 고통 **fling** 던지다 **ignore** 무시하다, 묵살하다 **upset** 당황한 **hurt** 다치게 하다, 아프게 하다 **wipe** 닦아 내다, 훔치다 **sweat** 땀 **punishment** 형벌, 징벌 **warn** 경고하다 **escape** 달아나다 **fate** 운명 **haunt** 유령이 붙어 다니다, 따라 다니다

described, Jacob?" he asked in a shaking voice.

"It is," replied the Ghost.

"I...I think I'd rather not," said Scrooge.

"Without their visits, you have no hope," warned the Ghost. "You will be like me. Expect the first tomorrow after the clock rings at one.

"Couldn't I just see them all at the same time and have it over, Jacob?" asked Scrooge.

"Expect the second on the next night at the same hour," said the Ghost. "The third will come on the next night when the last stroke* of twelve stops ringing. You will not see me anymore! But you must remember what I told you! It will help you if you want to save yourself."

When it said these words, the Ghost took its bandage from the table, and put it around its head, as before. Its teeth clicked* together as the Ghost put its jaw back where it should be. He slowly looked up again to see the Ghost standing with its chain wrapped around its arms.

The Ghost walked backward* from him. At every step it took, the window raised by itself a little. When the Ghost got to it, it was wide open. It called Scrooge to come closer, which he did. When they were two steps away from each other, Marley's Ghost held up its hand, warning him to come no nearer. Scrooge stopped.

Now that* he was this close to the Ghost, he heard many things. He heard the crying of many ghosts who regretted their wasted lives. He heard their pain and their fear. He heard the screams* of their suffering. This Ghost, after listening for a moment, began to scream as well

---

stroke 치는 소리, 울림 **click** 딸깍 소리가 나다 **backward** 뒤로 **now that** ~이니까, ~이기 때문에 **scream** 절규, 쇳소리

and floated out into the silent, dark night. Scrooge ran to the window, feeling very curious. He looked out.

The air was filled with* ghosts, wandering here and there quickly, and crying as they went. Every one of them wore chains like Marley's Ghost. Some of them were tied* to each other. Some of the chains were longer or shorter, but none of them were free. Scrooge recognized* some of their faces.

He had been quite familiar* with one old Ghost, in a white coat, with a tremendous* iron safe* attached* to its ankle.* It cried loudly because it could not help a living woman and her newborn baby* who were sitting outside one of the doors below. It was clear that the ghosts' greatest suffering was that they could only watch humans. They had lost the power to do anything to or with the living people forever.

Whether these creatures* faded* into mist, or the mist covered them, he could not tell. But they and their spirit voices faded together. The night again became silent.

Scrooge closed the window and looked at the door by which the Ghost had entered. It was double-locked,* as he had locked it with his own hands, and the locks looked unchanged. He tried to say "Humbug!" but stopped at the first sound. Because of how late it was, how fatigued* he felt from all the ghosts he had seen, and how scared* he was of his future, he very much needed rest. He went straight to bed, without changing his clothes, and fell asleep immediately.*

be filled with ~로 가득하다 **tie** 묶다 **recognize** 알아보다 **familiar** 친한 **tremendous** 거대한 **safe** 금고 **attached** 덧붙여진 **ankle** 발목 **newborn baby** 신생아 **creature** 산물, 생물 **fade** 사라지다 **double-lock** 이중으로 잠그다 **fatigued** 몹시 피곤한 **scared** 두려운 **immediately** 곧, 즉각

Chapter 02

The First of the Three Spirits

스크루지에게 첫 번째로 과거의 크리스마스 유령이 찾아온다.
유령은 스크루지를 과거로 데려가고, 그곳에서 스크루지는
천진난만하고 때 묻지 않은 자신의 어린 시절과 청년기의 모습을 만난다.

When Scrooge awoke,* it was so dark that he could barely see the window on his wall. He was trying to see in the dark when he heard the ringing of the bells in a church nearby. So he listened for the hour.

To his great astonishment, the heavy bell went on from six to seven, and from seven to eight, and regularly* up to twelve and then stopped. Twelve! It was past two when he went to bed. The clock was wrong. The ice must have broken the bell. Twelve! He looked on his desk for his own clock. Its quick little pulse* beat twelve and stopped.

"Why, it isn't possible that I could have slept through a whole day and far into another night," said Scrooge. "It isn't possible* that something has happened to the sun and this is at twelve noon!"

This idea was so shocking* that he jumped out of bed and felt his way to the window. He had to rub* the frost off with the sleeve* of his nightgown* before he could see anything and still saw very little. All he could see was that it was still

awake 잠에서 깨어나다 **regularly** 규칙적으로 **pulse** 맥박, 파동 **possible** 가능한 **shocking** 충격적인, 소름 끼치는 **rub** 비비다, 문지르다 **sleeve** 소매 **nightgown** 잠옷

very foggy and cold. There was no noise coming from people running here and there, though there definitely* would have been if it were daytime but still dark. This made Scrooge feel a little better. He couldn't imagine what would happen if the sun stopped shining!

Scrooge went to bed again and thought, and thought, and thought it over and over and over, but could not think of any reason. The more he thought, the more confused* he was. The more he tried not to think, the more he thought.

Marley's Ghost bothered him a lot. He could not stop thinking of its cold air or unmoving* eyes. Every time he told himself that it was only a dream, his mind kept wondering if it wasn't.

"Was it a dream or not?" he asked himself.

Scrooge lay in this state* until forty-five

minutes passed. Then he remembered, suddenly, that the Ghost had warned him that another Ghost was coming at one. He decided* to stay awake until the hour passed, which was easy because he did not think he could fall asleep anyway.

Those fifteen minutes were so long that he thought a few times that he must have fallen asleep and missed the clock. Finally the clock began to ring.

"The hour is up, and there is nothing else!" Scrooge said triumphantly.* He spoke before the hour bell sounded, deep and melancholy. Light flashed* up in the room instantly,* and the curtains of his bed opened.

The curtains of his bed were pulled aside by a hand. Neither did the curtains

definitely 확실히 **confused** 혼란스러운, 헛갈리는 **unmoving** 움직이지 않는 **state** 상태 **decide** 결심하다, 결정하다 **triumphantly** 의기양양하게 **flash** 번쩍 비치다, 번쩍거리다 **instantly** 즉시, 즉석에서

at his feet, nor did the curtains at his back, but his face was moved to those curtains. Scrooge sat up and faced the strange ghostly figure.*

It was a strange figure. It looked like both a child and an old man. Its hair, which hung around its neck and down its back, was white from age, and yet the face had no wrinkles.* Even its cheeks were a red, rosy color. The arms and hands were long and muscular.* It made the figure look especially* strong.

Its legs and feet looked delicate* and were not covered under clothing. It wore a pure* white shirt and around its waist was a beautiful, shining belt. It held a branch of fresh green holly* in its hand. The bottom* of its dress was decorated with* summer flowers.

But the strangest thing about it was that from the top of its head there shone a bright, clear light. It lit up the whole room. It also carried a cap that it could use to hide the light.

But as Scrooge stared at the figure, he realized that even this was not the strangest thing about it. At one moment, the belt sparkled and then it became dark. Suddenly it was a thing with one arm, now with onc leg, now with twenty legs, now a pair of legs without a head, now a head without a body. All these different parts disappeared into the darkness, and then it looked like itself again.

"Are you the Spirit, sir, who is supposed to visit me?" asked Scrooge.

"I am!" said the Spirit.

The voice was soft and gentle.* It sounded far away instead of close to him.

figure 형태, 형상 **wrinkle** 주름, 잔주름 **muscular** 근육의 **especially** 특히, 유달리 **delicate** 연약한, 가냘픈 **pure** 순수한 **holly** 서양호랑가시나무 **bottom** 밑바닥 **be decorated with** ~로 장식되다 **gentle** 상냥한, 부드러운

"Who and what are you?" asked Scrooge.

"I am the Spirit of Christmas Past," said the Spirit.

"Long Past?" asked Scrooge, because it looked like some magical* creature.

"No. Your past," said the Spirit.

Scrooge did not know why, but he suddenly wanted to see the Spirit put on its cap. He asked it to.

"What!" exclaimed* the Spirit. "Why don't you want to see the light that I give? Isn't it enough that you are one of those who helped make this cap? You are one of the reasons I have to carry and wear it sometimes."

"I have no idea what you are talking about," said Scrooge. "I never made any caps or ever met you before. Why are you here?"

"For you!" said the Spirit.

"Ah, thank you," Scrooge answered, but he was actually thinking that he would rather sleep. The Spirit must have heard him thinking.

"You must listen to me!" the Spirit said immediately.

It put out its strong hand as it spoke and clasped* him gently by the arm.

"Rise*!" said the Spirit. "And walk with me!"

Scrooge could have complained* that it was late at night. He could have complained that it was freezing outside and that he only had thin night clothes on and no shoes. But it would have been useless. Though the Spirit's hands were as gentle as a lady's, he could not resist* it. He stood up, but as they walked to the window, he stopped.

---

magical 신비한, 마법의 **exclaim** 외치다, 소리치다 **clasp** 꽉 쥐다 **rise** 일어서다 **complain** 불평하다, 투덜거리다 **resist** 저항하다

"I can't fly," Scrooge whispered. "I will fall."

"Don't worry," said the Spirit. "Trust* me. You will be able to fly!"

As the words were spoken, they passed through the wall and stood on an open country road with fields on both sides. The city had disappeared. The darkness and the mist had also disappeared with it, for it was a clear, cold, winter day with snow on the ground.

"Good Heaven!" said Scrooge, clasping his hands together, as he looked around him. "I grew up here! I was a boy here!"

The Spirit gazed at him quietly. Scrooge could still feel its gentle touch. He smelled a thousand different smells floating in the air. Each one was connected* with a thousand thoughts, and hopes, and joys, and cares long, long, forgotten!

"Your lip is shaking," said the Spirit.

"And what is that on your cheek?"

"It's just a pimple,*" Scrooge grumbled.

"Do you remember the way?" asked the Spirit.

"I remember it!" cried Scrooge with passion.* "I could walk there while wearing a blindfold.*"

"Then why did you forget it for so many years?" asked the Spirit. "Let's go on."

They walked along the road, and Scrooge recognized every gate, and post,* and tree. A little market town appeared* in the distance,* with its bridge, its church, and winding* river. Some shaggy* ponies* were walking toward them with boys on their backs who called to other boys in carts* driven by farmers. All these boys were very happy and shouted to each other

trust 믿다 **connect** 연결하다, 잇다 **pimple** 여드름, 뾰루지 **with passion** 열렬하게 **blindfold** 눈가리개, 눈속임 **post** 기둥, 말뚝 **appear** 나타나다, 나오다 **in the distance** 멀리서 **winding** 꾸불꾸불한 **shaggy** 털이 많은, 텁수룩한 **pony** 조랑말 **cart** 짐수레

until the broad* fields were full of merry music.

"These are but* shadows* of the things that have been," said the Spirit. "They do not know we are here."

As the people passed, Scrooge knew and called each one by name. He was so full of joy to see all of them! His cold eye sparkled, and his heart beat* quickly as they passed. Why was he filled with gladness* when he heard them give each other merry Christmases? What was merry Christmas to Scrooge? Go away merry Christmas! What good had it ever done to him?

"The school is not yet deserted,*" said the Spirit. "A lonely child, neglected* by his friends, is left there still."

Scrooge said he knew it. And he wept.*

They left the high road and entered a well-remembered road. Soon they approached a mansion* of dull* red brick.* There was a bell on the roof. It was a large house, but it looked sad. The large offices were little used, their walls were damp* and mossy,* their windows broken, and their gates rotten. Chickens made noise in the stables,* and the sheds* had long grass growing inside them.

It did not look any better inside. If someone entered, and looked into the rooms, he would have found them with only a few pieces of furniture, cold, and vast.* There was an earthy* smell in the chilly air.

The Spirit and Scrooge went across the hall to a door at the back of the house. It opened in front of them and showed a long, melancholy room with simple

broad 넓은 **but** 그저, 단지 ~뿐 **shadow** 환영 **beat** 뛰다, 고동치다 **gladness** 기쁨 **deserted** 인적이 끊긴 **neglect** 무시하다 **weep** 흐느끼다 **mansion** 대저택 **dull** 분명하지 않은 **brick** 벽돌 **damp** 축축한 **mossy** 이끼 낀 **stable** 마구간 **shed** 가축 우리, 창고 **vast** 거대한 **earthy** 흙의

desks and chairs. In one of these, a lonely-looking* boy was reading near a weak fire. Scrooge sat down and wept to see his poor forgotten self* as he used to be.

Not a squeak* from the mice behind the walls, not a drip from the water faucet* outside, not a wind in the leafless* trees outside, not a sound from a swinging door or a clicking* in the fire could comfort* Scrooge as he wept.

The Spirit touched him on the arm and pointed to* his younger self, who was still reading. Suddenly a man in foreign* clothes, which were wonderfully* real, stood outside the window. He had an ax* stuck* in his belt and was leading a donkey.*

"Why, it's Ali Baba!" Scrooge exclaimed. "It's dear, old, honest Ali Baba! Yes, I know! One Christmas day, when that lonely child was left here all alone, he came for the first time. Poor boy! And Valentine and his wild brother, Orson! There they go! And what's his name? The man who was killed in his sleep! Don't you see him? I'm glad he was! How could he marry Princess?"

To hear Scrooge talking about Ali Baba and other fairy tales* while he was laughing and crying would have shocked the other businessmen.

"There's the Parrot* with its green body and yellow tail and a thing that looks like lettuce* growing out of the top of his head. There he is! Poor Robinson Crusoe! When he came home again after sailing around the island,* the Parrot said, 'Poor Robinson Crusoe, where have you been,

lonely-looking 외로워 보이는 **self** 자아, 자기 **squeak** 찍찍 울다 **faucet** 수도꼭지 **leafless** 잎이 없는 **clicking** 딸깍거리는 **comfort** 위안하다, 위로하다 **point to** ~을 가리키다, 지적하다 **foreign** 외국의 **wonderfully** 이상하게도, 놀랄 만큼 **ax** 도끼 **stick** 찔러 넣다, 꽂다 **donkey** 당나귀 **fairy tale** 동화, 옛날이야기 **parrot** 앵무새 **lettuce** 상추, 양상추 **island** 섬

Robinson Crusoe?' The man thought he was dreaming, but he wasn't. Oh, there goes Friday, running for his life, to the little river!"

Scrooge felt pity for his childhood.*

"Poor boy!" he cried again.

Quickly his whole face changed, and he no longer looked excited. Instead, he looked sad.

"It's too late now," Scrooge grumbled quietly and put his hands in his pockets.

"What is the matter?" asked the Spirit.

"Nothing," said Scrooge. "Nothing. There was a boy singing a Christmas carol at my door last night. I wish I had given him something. That's all."

"Let's see another Christmas," said the Spirit as it smiled thoughtfully* and waved* its hand.

Scrooge's younger self grew larger as soon as it said these words, and the room became a little darker and dirtier. The wood on the walls became smaller, the windows cracked,* and pieces of the ceiling* fell down. There he was, alone again, when all the other boys had gone home for the jolly* holidays.

The boy was not reading now but walking up and down, upset. Scrooge looked at the Spirit, and with a sad shaking of his head, looked anxiously* toward the door. It opened, and a little girl, much younger than the boy, came running in. She put her arms around his neck and kissed him.

"Dear, dear brother," she said to him, clapping her tiny hands and bending down* to laugh. "I have come to bring you home, dear brother! To bring you home,

childhood 어린 시절, 유년 시절 **thoughtfully** 생각에 잠겨, 사려 깊게 **wave** 흔들다 **crack** 금이 가다 **ceiling** 천장 **jolly** 즐거운, 유쾌한 **anxiously** 근심하여, 걱정스럽게 **bend down** 상체를 구부리다

home, home!"

"Home, little Fan?" said the boy.

"Yes!" said the girl, full of happiness. "Home, for good.* Home, forever and ever. Father is so much kinder than he used to be. Home's like Heaven! He spoke so gently to me one dear night when I was going to bed that I was not afraid to ask him again if you could come home. He said, 'Yes, you should.' He sent me in a carriage* to bring you. And you're to be a man! You will never come back here, but first, we're going to be together all Christmas and have the merriest time in the world."

"You are quite a woman, little Fan!" exclaimed the boy.

She clapped her hands and laughed. She tried to touch his head, but she was too little. She laughed again and stood up to embrace* him. Then she began to pull him eagerly* toward the door. He happily followed her.

"Bring down Scrooge's box, there!" a terrible* voice cried in the hall. In the hall appeared the schoolmaster* himself, who stared at Scrooge scarily.* He shook hands with Scrooge, which made him really nervous.*

The schoolmaster then brought him and his sister into a very fancy* and important-looking room, where the maps on the wall and globes* by the window looked fake* and cold. Here he took out a bottle of wine that was strangely light and a piece of cake that was strangely heavy. He told the young people to eat.

Scrooge's trunk* was finally tied up to be carried away. The children happily

for good 영원히 **carriage** 사륜마차 **embrace** 포옹하다, 껴안다 **eagerly** 열심히, 간절히 **terrible** 소름끼치는, 무시무시한 **schoolmaster** 교장 **scarily** 겁나게, 놀라게 **nervous** 초조한, 긴장한 **fancy** 화려한 **globe** 지구본 **fake** 가짜의, 모조의 **trunk** 여행용 큰 가방, 트렁크

said goodbye to the schoolmaster and left the room. They got into the carriage and drove happily down past the garden. The wheels and the horse's hooves* splashed* the water as the carriage ran through the street.

"She was always so weak," said the Spirit. "But she had a large heart!"

"Yes, she did!" cried Scrooge. "You're right. I will not disagree,* Spirit!"

"She died a woman and had, as I think, children," said the Spirit.

"One child," said Scrooge.

"True," said the Spirit. "Your nephew!"

"Yes," replied Scrooge briefly.* He seemed uncomfortable* in his mind.

Although they had just left the school behind them, they were now in the busy streets of a city. There, shadowy passers-by* passed and shadowy carts and coaches* battled for* the way. It was truly complicated* and dirty. Because of the decorations* in the shops, it was clear that here too it was Christmas time again. It was evening, and the streets were lit up.*

The Spirit stopped at a certain warehouse* door and asked Scrooge if he knew it.

"I know it?" said Scrooge. "I learned how to be a businessman here!"

They went in. They saw an old man wearing a wig* sitting in a chair that looked too small for his tall stature.*

"Why, it's old Fezziwig!" cried Scrooge. "Bless his heart! It's Fezziwig alive again!"

Old Fezziwig laid down* his pen and looked up at the clock, which pointed to the hour of seven. He rubbed his hands

hoof 발굽 **splash** 튀기다 **disagree** 의견이 다르다 **briefly** 짧게, 간단하게 **uncomfortable** 마음이 편하지 못한, 거북한 **passer-by** 행인 **coach** 대형 사륜마차 **battle for** ~을 위해 투쟁하다, 싸우다 **complicated** 복잡한, 뒤얽힌 **decoration** 장식(물) **light up** 불을 밝히다 **warehouse** 상점, 창고 **wig** 가발, 머리 장식 **stature** 키 **lay down** 내려놓다

and fixed* his coat. He laughed from all over himself.

"Yo ho, there! Ebenezer! Dick!" he called out in a voice that was comfortable, oily,* and joyful. Scrooge's former self, now a grown young man, came quickly in, followed by the other apprentice.*

"That's Dick Wilkins!" said Scrooge to the Spirit. "Bless me, yes. There he is. He really liked me. Poor Dick! Dear!"

"Yo ho, my boys!" said Fezziwig. "No more work tonight. Christmas Eve, Dick. Christmas, Ebenezer! Let's close the windows."

You wouldn't believe how quickly they went! They ran into the street with the shutters*—one, two, three—, had them up in their places—four, five, six—closed them—seven, eight, and nine. They came back breathing like race horses.

"That's right!" cried old Fezziwig,

jumping down from the high desk. "Clear the room, my boys, and let's have lots of room here! Come on, Dick! Let's go, Ebenezer!"

Clear the room! There was nothing they wouldn't have cleared away, or couldn't have cleared away, with old Fezziwig watching. It was done in a minute. Everything movable* was packed away, as if no one would need it anymore. The floor was swept and watered, the lamps were turned on, and firewood* was piled on the fire. The warehouse was so comfortable, warm, dry, and bright a ballroom.*

In came a fiddler,* with a music book. He got on the top of a desk and began playing. In came Mrs. Fezziwig, with

fix 매만지다, 가다듬다 **oily** 알랑거리는, 넉살 좋은 **apprentice** 도제, 견습생 **shutter** 셔터, 덧문 **movable** 움직일 수 있는 **firewood** 장작 **ballroom** 무도회장 **fiddler** 바이올리니스트

her vast smile. In came the three Miss Fezziwigs, smiling and lovable.* In came the six young men, whose hearts they broke.

In came all the young men and women employed* in the business. In came the housemaid,* with her cousin, the baker. In came the cook, with her brother's close friend, the milkman.* In came the boy from over the way, who was not paid enough by his boss. He was trying to hide himself behind the girl from next door.

In they all came, one after another,* some shyly, some boldly,* some gracefully,* some awkwardly,* some pushing, some pulling. In they all came in every way they could. When they all came in, there were twenty couples. They all tried to dance together in big groups and lines. Sometimes they messed up* and looked strange. Other times, they danced perfectly.

When they finally danced perfectly, old Fezziwig clapped his hands to stop the dance.

"Well done!" he cried out. The fiddler put his hot face into a pot of water. He did not rest and instantly began to play again, though there were no dancers yet.

There were more dances, and there was cake, and there were drinks, and there was a great chunk* of beef, and there was a great piece of fish, and there were pies, and lots of beer. But the best part of the evening came after the dinner. This was when the fiddler began playing a very popular song.

Then old Fezziwig began to dance with Mrs. Fezziwig. They were the best couple

lovable 사랑스러운 **employ** 고용하다 **housemaid** 가정부, 하녀 **milkman** 우유 장수, 우유 배달인 **one after another** 차례차례 **boldly** 대담하게, 뻔뻔스럽게 **gracefully** 우아하게 **awkwardly** 어색하게, 서투르게 **mess up** 실수하다, 엉망진창을 만들다 **chunk** 덩어리

dancing, too. They danced better than all of the young people. They were the kind of people who could dance better than they could walk.

Even if the number of dancers had doubled,* old Fezziwig would still have been better than them and so would Mrs. Fezziwig. As to her, she was as good a dancer as he was. A beautiful light seemed to come from Fezziwig's legs. They shone in every part of the dance like moons. You couldn't have guessed* what they were going to do next. And when old Fezziwig and Mrs. Fezziwig had finished the dance, Fezziwig jumped up high and landed* perfectly.

When the clock struck eleven, the party ended. Mr. and Mrs. Fezziwig stood on either side of the door and shook hands with every person individually* as he or she went out. They also wished him or her a merry Christmas. When everybody left but the two apprentices, they did the same to them. Thus the cheerful voices died away.* The boys went to their beds, which were under a counter* in the back of the shop.

During all of this time, Scrooge had been very excited. His heart and soul were with his younger self. He thought about everything, remembered everything, enjoyed everything, and felt strangely annoyed.* It was not until now, when the bright faces of his former self and Dick were turned, that he remembered the Spirit and realized that it was looking at him while the light on its head was very clear.

"It seems very easy to make these silly

double 두 배가 되다 **guess** 짐작하다, 추측하다 **land** 착지하다, 땅에 내려서다 **individually** 개인적으로, 개별적으로 **die away** 잦아들다, 약해지다 **counter** 계산대, 카운터 **annoyed** 짜증나는, 화가 난

people happy," said the Spirit.

"Easy!" said Scrooge.

The Spirit pointed at the two apprentices, who were praising* Fezziwig.

"Why, is it not?" said the Spirit. "He has spent only a little money on this party. Why does he deserve* so much praise?"

"It isn't that," said Scrooge, feeling angry, like his younger self, not his older self. "It isn't that, Spirit. The old Fezziwig has the power to make us happy or unhappy, to make our work light or burdensome* and to make us have pleasure or suffer. His power is in words and looks. It is in things so slight and small, so it is impossible to add and count them. The happiness he gives is the same as a fortune.*"

He felt the Spirit's stare and stopped.

"What is the matter?" asked the Spirit.

"Nothing," said Scrooge.

"Something, I think?" continued the Spirit.

"No," said Scrooge. "I wish I could say something to my clerk just now. That's all."

His younger self turned down* the lamps as he said goodnight. Scrooge and the Spirit again stood side by side* in the open air.

"My time grows short," said the Spirit. "Quick!"

This was not said to Scrooge, or to any one whom he could see, but everything changed immediately. Again Scrooge saw himself. He was older now. He was now an adult* man. His face did not have deep wrinkles or spots.* But it did have signs* of greed.* There was something

praise 칭찬하다 **deserve** ~할 만하다, ~할 가치가 있다 **burdensome** 부담이 되는, 귀찮은 **fortune** 재산, 큰 재물 **turn down** 낮추다, 줄이다 **side by side** 나란히 **adult** 어른, 성인 **spot** 반점, 검버섯 **sign** 징조, 조짐 **greed** 탐욕, 큰 욕심

eager and greedy in his eye. It showed that the passion* for money had taken root* and the shadow of the growing tree of selfishness* in his heart.

He was not alone, but sat by the side of a pretty young girl in a black dress. There were tears in her eyes, which sparkled in the light that shone out of the Spirit of Christmas Past.

"It matters* little," she said softly. "To you, very little. Something else has replaced* me. If it can cheer and comfort you in the future, as I have tried to do, I have no good reason to be sad."

"What has replaced you?" he asked.

"A golden idol,*" she replied.

"This is ridiculous!" he said. "Do you know how hard it is to be poor? There is nothing wrong with wanting to be rich!"

"You fear the world too much," she said, gently. "All your other hopes have combined* into the hope of being rich. I have seen your noble* hopes die, one by one, until only your greed remained."

"What then?" he said. "I have grown much wiser, haven't I? I am not changed toward you."

She shook her head.

"Am I?" he asked.

"Our relationship* is an old one," she said. "It was made when we were both poor and happy to be so, until things changed. We could improve* our worldly fortune by our doing hard work patiently.* You are changed. When it was made, you were another man."

"I was a boy," he said impatiently.*

"You know deep in your heart that

---

passion 열정 **take root** 뿌리를 내리다 **selfishness** 이기심 **matter** 문제가 되다, 중요하다 **replace** 대신하다, 대체하다 **idol** 우상 **combine** 결합시키다, 합치다 **noble** 고귀한, 훌륭한 **relationship** 관계, 관련 **improve** 개선하다, 증진하다 **patiently** 참을성 있게 **impatiently** 조급하게, 참지 못하고

you have changed," she said. "I am sure. The things that made us happy when we shared the same heart will not make us happy now. We are two hearts again. How often and how keenly* I have thought of this, I will not say. But I have thought about it, and it's time to let you go."

"Have I ever asked you to let me go?" he asked.

"In words, no" she said. "Never."

"In what, then?" he asked.

"You have asked me with a changed nature,* a changed spirit, another atmosphere* of life, and another hope," she said as she stared at him. "You don't need my love now. It's not important to you now. If we had not started our relationship years ago, tell me, would you seek me out and try to marry me now? Ah, no!"

"You should not think like that!" he

cried. Even though he did not want to agree with her, part of him knew it was true.

"I would gladly think otherwise* if I could," she said. "Heaven knows! When I have learned a truth like this, I know how strong it must be. I cannot forget it. But if you were free today, tomorrow, yesterday, how could I believe that you would choose a poor girl? Why would you choose a girl who would bring you no money? If you did choose her, I know how much you would regret it. I know that if you met me today, you would not want me. So, I'm letting you go. I let you go with a full heart* because I love the man that you used to be."

He was about to* speak, but with her

keenly 날카롭게, 예민하게 **nature** 성격, 본성 **atmosphere** 분위기, 환경
otherwise 다르게, 이와는 반대로 **with a full heart** 진심으로, 온 마음을 다해
be about to 막 ~하려고 하다

head turned from him, she resumed.*

"You may feel pain because of this," she said. "A part of me hopes you do feel bad because of my good memories. You will only feel bad for a short time. Then you will think that our time together was a silly dream. May you be happy in the life you have chosen!"

She left him, and they parted.*

"Spirit!" said Scrooge, "Show me no more! Bring me home. Why do you enjoy torturing me?"

"One shadow more!" exclaimed the Spirit.

"No more!" cried Scrooge. "No more. I don't wish to see it. Show me no more!"

But the Spirit grabbed both his arms and forced* him to watch what happened next.

They were in another place, a room, not very large or handsome, but full of comfort. Near the winter fire sat a beautiful young girl. She looked so much like the young woman that had left Scrooge. Not until did he see an older woman sitting opposite her than he realized that the young girl was her daughter. The noise in this room was perfectly loud, for there were more children there, than Scrooge could count. They ran around screaming, playing, and jumping.

It was so noisy, but no one seemed to care. Instead, the mother and daughter laughed and enjoyed it very much. The daughter started playing with the children. The children attacked* and played with her happily. They teased* her and wrapped their arms around her waist.

Then a knocking at the door was

---

resume 다시 시작하다 **part** 헤어지다 **force** 억지로 ~시키다, 강요하다
attack 공격하다, 습격하다 **tease** 괴롭히다, 곯리다

heard, and immediately all the children ran to the door to greet their father, who came in with another man who held Christmas toys and presents. The children shouted and started jumping on the poor, defenseless* man! They climbed* on chairs and stuck their hands in his pockets. They pulled candy and toys out of paper bags. They hugged* him around his neck, punched* his back, and kicked his legs!

They shouted in wonder* and delight as they opened each package*! Suddenly, someone exclaimed that the baby had eaten the doll's frying pan. They saw the baby put it in its mouth and they knew it had disappeared! Everyone felt better when they found the frying pan somewhere* else! There was joy and happiness! They could not describe how happy they were. It took a long time, but finally the children calmed down* and were quiet again. Late that night, they went to sleep.

And now Scrooge looked on more closely* than ever. The father, while his daughter leaned* fondly* on him, sat down with her and her mother. At that moment, Scrooge realized that this graceful, special, interesting girl might have called him father instead of this man. She could have made winter feel like spring. His heart grew very heavy.

"Honey,* I saw an old friend of yours this afternoon," said the husband, turning to his wife with a smile.

"Who was it?" asked the wife.

"Guess!" said the husband.

"How can I?" she said, laughing as he laughed. "Mr. Scrooge."

defenseless 무방비의, 방어할 수 없는 **climb** 오르다, 기어오르다 **hug** 꼭 껴안다 **punch** 강타하다, 일격을 가하다 **wonder** 경이, 경탄 **package** 꾸러미, 소포 **somewhere** 어딘가에 **calm down** 진정하다, 차분하다 **closely** 자세히 **lean** 기대다, 기대서다 **fondly** 다정하게 **honey** 여보, 당신

"Mr. Scrooge it was," said the husband. "I passed his office window. Because it was not closed, and he had a candle inside, I could see him. His partner is almost dead, I hear. There he sat, alone. Quite alone in the world, I do believe."

"Spirit!" said Scrooge in a broken voice. "Take me away from this place."

"I told you these were shadows of the things that have been," said the Spirit. "That they are what they are. Do not become angry at me!"

"Take me away!" Scrooge exclaimed, "I cannot watch it!"

He turned to the Spirit. When he looked at the Spirit's face, he saw the faces of all the people he had just seen in its face.

"Leave me!" he cried. "Take me back. Haunt me no longer!"

The Spirit held onto* Scrooge while he struggled. Nothing Scrooge did seemed to bother the Spirit at all. It only looked at Scrooge gently. Scrooge saw that its light was burning high and bright. He realized that the light was what was showing him all these things. He grabbed the cap and suddenly pressed it down* upon its head.

The Spirit shrank* beneath it so that the cap covered its whole body. Though Scrooge pressed it down with all his strength,* he could not hide the light. It streamed out* from under it in an unbroken* flood* upon the ground.

He realized that he was very tired and that he was in his own bedroom. He gave the cap a final squeeze.* Then he relaxed* and barely had time to go to bed before he fell into a heavy sleep.

hold onto ~을 꼭 잡고 있다 **press down** 내리누르다 **shrink** 줄어들다 **with all one's strength** 힘껏, 온 힘을 다해 **stream out** 흘러 나오다 **unbroken** 끊어지지 않은 **flood** 홍수, 범람 **squeeze** 압착, 짓누름 **relax** 긴장이 풀리다, 나른해지다

Chapter 03

The Second of the Three Spirits

스크루지에게 현재의 크리스마스 유령이 찾아온다.
스크루지는 유령을 따라 자신의 서기인 밥 크래칫을 방문하고
그의 어렵게 사는 모습에 동정을 느끼며, 조카인 프레드의 집에서는
자신을 변함없이 사랑해주는 조카의 마음씨에 감동한다.

Awaking in the middle of a very loud snore,* and sitting up in bed to get his thoughts together, Scrooge knew that the next Spirit would come soon. He thought that he had woken up at the right time in order to meet the second Spirit that was expected to come to him.

He became uncomfortably cold as he began to wonder which one of his curtains the Spirit would open. He decided to open all of them. He wished to greet the Spirit as soon as he saw it. He did not want to be surprised or nervous.

There are some men who are very relaxed* and tolerant.* They can see all kinds of strange things and not care. Scrooge was not so tolerant, now his mind had changed a little. At that night at that moment, Scrooge was ready to see anything, even if it were as strange as a baby riding* a rhinoceros.*

Now, because he was prepared for almost anything, he was not at all prepared for nothing. So, when the bell struck one, and no shape* appeared, he began to shake and shiver. Five minutes, ten minutes, a

---

snore 코골기 **relaxed** 느긋한 **tolerant** 관대한, 인내심 있는 **ride** 타다, 타고 가다 **rhinoceros** 무소, 코뿔소 **shape** 형태, 형상

quarter of an hour went by, yet nothing came. All this time, he lay upon his bed.

The red light which came into his room when the clock struck the next hour was more frightening than a dozen ghosts. He was powerless* to understand it. He began to fear that he might suddenly catch on fire* without knowing it.

At last, however, he began to think that this ghostly light might be coming from the next room. When he looked more carefully, he realized that it seemed to shine from there. When he decided this idea was true, he quietly got up, put on his slippers, and walked there.

The moment* Scrooge's hand was on the door, a strange voice called him by his name and told him to enter. He entered.

It was his own room. There was no doubt* about that. But there had been a surprising change. The walls and ceiling were decorated by living green plants. The room looked like a perfect garden. From every part of the garden, bright shining berries* grew. The fresh leaves of holly, mistletoe,* and ivy* reflected* back the light, as if so many little mirrors* had been scattered* on them. A great fire was roaring* in the fireplace. The fireplace had not had such a big fire since long before Marley or Scrooge had lived in the house.

Piled up on the floor, in the shape of a king's throne,* were turkey,* geese, deer, chicken, beef, pork, and long strings* of sausages. On top of that were meat pies, plum* puddings, barrels* of oysters,* and red-hot chestnuts.* There were also apples, juicy oranges, tasty pears, huge cakes, and

powerless 무력한, 무능한 **catch on fire** 불붙다 **the moment** ~하는 순간 **doubt** 의심, 회의 **berry** 베리(딸기류의 열매) **mistletoe** 겨우살이 **ivy** 담쟁이덩굴 **reflect** 반사하다, 반향하다 **mirror** 거울, 반사경 **scatter** 흩뿌리다, 흩어 버리다 **roar** 으르렁거리다 **throne** 왕좌, 옥좌 **turkey** 칠면조(고기) **string** 한 줄 **plum** 서양자두 **barrel** 통 **oyster** 굴 **chestnut** 밤

bowls of punch.* The whole room smelled of delicious food.

Sitting on this chair, there was a jolly Giant, wonderful to see. He held up high a glowing* torch* in the shape of a horn.* The light fell on Scrooge as he entered the room.

"Come in!" exclaimed the Spirit. "Come closer, man!"

Scrooge entered timidly* and bowed to this Spirit. He was not the tough* Scrooge he had been, and though the Spirit's eyes were clear and kind, he did not like to meet them.

"I am the Spirit of Christmas Present," said the Spirit. "Look at me!"

Scrooge looked at it as if it were a king. It was clothed in a simple green robe* with white fur.* This garment* hung so loosely* on its body, that its strong chest was bare.* Its feet, underneath the bottom of the long robe, were also bare. On its head, it wore a holly wreath* with shining icicles.* Its dark brown curls* were long and free. Its face was gentle. Its sparkling eye, its open hand, its cheery* voice, and its joyful air were all free. Around its waist a scabbard,* but it was empty with no sword.*

"You have never seen something like me before!" exclaimed the Spirit.

"Never," replied Scrooge.

"Have you never walked with my brothers?" continued the Spirit. "I am very young, you know."

"I don't think I have," said Scrooge. "I am afraid I have not. Have you had many brothers, Spirit?"

"More than eighteen hundred," said the

---

punch 펀치(음료) **glowing** 작열하는, 시뻘건 **torch** 횃불 **horn** 뿔 **timidly** 주뼛주뼛 **tough** 불굴의, 완고한 **robe** 로브(길고 헐거운 겉옷) **fur** 모피, 털 **garment** 의복 **loosely** 느슨하게, 헐겁게 **bare** 살을 드러낸, 맨살의 **wreath** 화관, 화환 **icicle** 은박지 등의 장식; 고드름 **curl** 곱슬거리는 머리카락, 곱슬거리게 만 것 **cheery** 기분 좋은, 쾌활한 **scabbard** 칼집, 검집 **sword** 검, 칼

Spirit.

"A tremendous family to feed*!" grumbled Scrooge.

The Spirit of Christmas Present rose.

"Spirit, bring me wherever you want," said Scrooge. "Last night, the Spirit made me go, and I learned a lesson* which I understand now. Tonight, if you have something to teach me, let me learn it."

"Touch my robe!" said the Spirit.

Scrooge did as he was told and held it tightly.*

Holly, mistletoe, red berries, ivy, turkey, geese, chicken, beef, pork, sausages, oysters, pies, puddings, fruit, and punch, all disappeared instantly. So did the room, the fire, the red glow, the hour of night, and they stood in the city streets on Christmas morning. It had snowed the night before, so people made loud noises as they swept* the snow from their houses.

It delighted the children to watch the snow fall off the houses.

The house fronts looked black, and the windows blacker because of the smooth white sheet of snow on the roofs and the dirty snow on the ground. The wheels of carriages and horses had made it dirty and made complicated patterns of yellow snow and mud.* The sky was gloomy,* and the shortest streets had a dirty mist and they were half melted, half frozen. There was nothing very cheerful in the weather or the town, and yet there was an air of cheerfulness,* as if it were a beautiful sunny day.

The people who were shoveling away* on the tops of the house were joyful. They called out to each other and threw

---

feed 먹이다 **lesson** 교훈 **tightly** 단단히, 꽉 **sweep** 청소하다, 쓸어 버리다 **mud** 진흙, 진창 **gloomy** 어두운, 음침한 **cheerfulness** 명랑함, 쾌활함 **shovel away** 삽으로 퍼내다

snowballs* and laughed happily if they hit someone or if they didn't. The chicken shops were still half open, and the fruit shops looked bright and beautiful in the snow. There were great, round baskets of chestnuts, shaped like the coats of jolly old gentlemen. They sat in front of doors or spilled* into the streets. There were red and brown-faced, Spanish* onions, shining like fat Spanish monks.*

There were pears and apples, grouped* high in blooming* pyramids.* There were bunches* of grapes hanging from shops. People's mouths watered* as they walked past. There were smells that reminded people of* ancient walks in the woods and playing in the brown leaves. There were even bright oranges and lemons. They looked so tasty* that they made people want to take them home in paper bags and eat them after dinner.

The gold and silver fish, sitting among these bright fruits in a bowl, seemed to know that it was a special day. They swam in circles in their slow excitement. But it was the grocery store that was the most wonderful place to go! The noise of the cans and the papers made a pleasant music.

The mixed smells of tea and coffee were so good. The raisins* were so delicious, the almonds* so white, and the sticks of cinnamon* so long and straight. The other spices* also looked delicious. The candied* fruits were covered in sweet liquid* sugar. The figs were moist,* and the French plums were both bitter* and sweet.

---

snowball 눈덩이 **spill** 넘치다, 엎지르다 **Spanish** 스페인의, 스페인 사람의 **monk** 수도사 **group** 무리를 짓다 **blooming** 번성한, 융성한 **pyramid** 피라미드 **bunch** 다발, 묶음 **water** 침이 생기다, 침을 흘리다 **remind A of B** A에게 B를 생각나게 하다 **tasty** 맛있는 **raisin** 건포도 **almond** 아몬드 **cinnamon** 계피 **spice** 양념 **candied** 설탕에 절인 **liquid** 액체 **moist** 촉촉한, 습한 **bitter** 쓴

The customers were all so hurried and so eager because of the special day. They bumped* into each other at the door, crashed* their baskets, and left their purchases* on the counter. Then they came running back to get them. They made hundreds of little mistakes, happily. In the meantime, the people who worked there looked especially clean and professional.*

But soon the bells rang and called good people all to church and chapel.* Away they went, crowding* through the streets in their best clothes and with their happiest faces. At the same time, people came out carrying their dinners to the baker's shops.

These people seemed to interest the Spirit very much. With his torch, he sprinkled something onto their food. And it was a very special kind of torch. Once or twice, when there was arguing* between some people who had pushed each other, he shed* a few drops of water on them from it. Then they were suddenly happy again. They said that it was a shame* to argue on Christmas Day.

In time, the bells stopped, and the bakers closed their shops. But the food was still cooking and melting the snow around the ovens.

"Is there a special taste in what you sprinkle from your torch?" asked Scrooge.

"There is," said the Spirit. "My own."

"Would it apply to* any kind of dinner on this day?" asked Scrooge.

"It would apply to any dinner that is kindly given," replied the Spirit. "Especially if it's given to a poor person."

bump 부딪치다, 충돌하다 **crash** 와장창 부수다 **purchase** 구입품, 산 물건 **professional** 직업의, 직업상의 **chapel** 예배당 **crowd** 군집하다, 모여들다 **arguing** 언쟁하기, 말다툼하기 **shed** 흘리다 **shame** 치욕, 수치 **apply to** ~에 적용되다, 해당되다

"Why to a poor one most?" asked Scrooge.

"Because he needs it most," said the Spirit.

"Spirit, I wonder why you should give the people less days to enjoy things," said Scrooge.

"I!" cried the Spirit.

"You would take away their meals every Sunday," said Scrooge, "and that is the only day they aren't working! Isn't it true?"

"I!" cried the Spirit.

"You close these shops on Sunday?" said Scrooge. "And then they have no rest or happiness."

"I close them!" exclaimed the Spirit.

"Forgive me if I am wrong," said Scrooge. "It has been done in your name or at least in that of your family."

"There are some people who do evil, prideful,* and selfish* things in our name," said the Spirit. "They are strange as to us. Remember that, and get angry at them, not us."

Scrooge promised that he would, and they went on, invisible, into the suburbs* of the town. Even though the Spirit was huge, Scrooge realized it could fit* itself into any place easily. It stood beneath a low roof quite as gracefully as it could have done in any hall with a high ceiling.

Perhaps the Spirit wanted to show its power, or it felt sorry for poor men. It led Scrooge straight to his clerk's house. It took Scrooge inside with it, holding onto its robe. In front of the door, the Spirit smiled and stopped to bless Bob Cratchit's house with the sprinkling of its torch. Think of that! Bob was so poor, but the Christmas Spirit blessed his house!

---

prideful 교만한, 건방진 **selfish** 이기적인, 제멋대로 하는 **suburbs** 교외, 시외
fit 맞다, 적합하다

Then up rose Mrs. Cratchit, Cratchit's wife, dressed in cheap clothing. Her dress was covered in pretty Christmas ribbons. She had made the dress with help from Belinda Cratchit, second of her daughters, who was also wearing ribbons. Master Peter Cratchit put his fork into a pot of potatoes. He was wearing a shirt that was too big. But his father had given it to him as a Christmas present. He wished Peter could go to the park to show off* his new fashion.*

And now two smaller Cratchits, a boy and girl, came running in, screaming that they had smelled the goose. They wanted to eat it. Loving the smells of sage* and onion, these young Cratchits danced around the table. They praised Master Peter Cratchit and called him handsome. While they danced, he smiled and continued to boil the potatoes in the pot.

"Where is your father?" said Mrs. Cratchit. "And your brother, Tiny Tim! And Martha wasn't a half an hour late last Christmas!"

"Here's Martha, Mother!" said a girl, appearing as she spoke.

"Here's Martha, Mother!" cried the two young Cratchits. "Hurrah! There's a goose, Martha!"

"Why, bless your heart, my dear, how late you are!" said Mrs. Cratchit, kissing her a dozen times and eagerly taking off her coat and hat.

"We had a lot of work to finish last night," replied the girl. "And we had to clean up the snow this morning, Mother!"

"Well, never mind!" said Mrs. Cratchit. "I'm just happy that you came. Sit down before the fire, my dear, and get warm.

---

show off 자랑하다 **fashion** 패션 **sage** 샐비어(식물)

Lord bless you!"

"No, no!" cried the two young Cratchits. "There's Father coming. Hide, Martha, hide!"

So Martha hid herself, and in came little Bob, the father, with his blanket wrapped around his thin body. He had tried to clean his poor clothes so that they looked nice for Christmas. Tiny Tim was lying on his shoulder. Alas for Tiny Tim, he could not walk without a crutch*!

"Why, where's our Martha?" cried Bob Cratchit, looking around.

"Not coming," said Mrs. Cratchit.

"Not coming!" said Bob, who suddenly looked sad. He had run so quickly home from church with Tim on his back. "Not coming on Christmas Day!"

Martha didn't like to see him disappointed, even in joke. So she came out early from behind the closet door and ran into his arms. The two young Cratchits carried Tiny Tim and took him off to his bath.

"And how was Tiny Tim at church?" asked Mrs. Cratchit, as Bob hugged his daughter happily.

"He was as good as gold.*" said Bob. "Somehow* he gets thoughtful,* sitting by himself so long, and thinks the strangest things you ever heard. He told me, coming home, that he hoped the people saw him in the church, because he was a cripple.* He hoped it would make them remember how Jesus made blind* men see and crippled men walk."

Bob's voice shook when he told them this and shook more when he said that Tiny Tim was growing strong and healthy.

crutch 목발 **as good as gold** (어린아이가) 아주 착한, 얌전한 **somehow** 어쨌지, 웬일인지 **thoughtful** 생각이 깊은, 사려 깊은 **cripple** 절름발이, 불구자 **blind** 눈먼, 장님인

They heard his crutch on the floor and back came Tiny Tim with his brother and sister. They put him on his stool in front of the fire. Bob made something hot in a jug with gin* and lemons, and stirred* it round and round and put it on the stove* to simmer.* Master Peter and the two young Cratchits went to get the goose. They soon returned with it.

All of them became so excited when they saw the goose. Mrs. Cratchit made the gravy,* which was still hot. Master Peter mashed* the potatoes eagerly. Belinda sweetened up* the apple sauce. Martha cleaned the hot plates.* Bob took Tiny Tim beside him in a tiny corner at the table.

The two young Cratchits set chairs for everybody, not forgetting themselves. Finally they pushed spoons into their mouths. They did not want other people to eat all of the goose. At last the dishes were filled with food, and everyone prayed.*

It was followed by a breathless* pause,* as Mrs. Cratchit, looking slowly at the knife, prepared to cut the goose. When she did, the stuffing* came out from the inside. Everyone smiled in delight all around the table. Even Tiny Tim, excited by the two young Cratchits, hit on the table with his knife and weakly cried Hurrah!

There never was such a goose. Bob said he didn't believe there ever was such a goose cooked. Its taste, size, and cheapness,* were what everyone praised. Along with apple sauce and mashed potatoes, it was a good dinner for the whole family.

gin 진 **stir** 휘젓다, 뒤섞다 **stove** 스토브, 난로 **simmer** 부글부글 끓다, 지글지글 끓다 **gravy** 육즙, 고기 국물 **mash** 짓찧다, 으깨다 **sweeten up** 달게 하다 **hot plate** 요리용 철판 **pray** 기도하다, 기원하다 **breathless** 숨죽인, 숨을 쉬지 않는 **pause** 중지, 중단 **stuffing** (음식의) 소, 내용물 **cheapness** 싼값, 염가

Indeed, as Mrs. Cratchit said with great delight, they were not able to finish it! Yet everyone had had enough. The youngest Cratchits had eaten piles of sage and onions! But now, the plates were being taken away by Belinda. Mrs. Cratchit left the room alone to get the pudding and bring it to the table. She was so nervous!

What if it was not cooked enough? What if it was cooked too much? What if someone stole it? All sorts of horrors were imagined*! It was so hot! The pudding was out of the oven. In half a minute Mrs. Cratchit entered, smiling proudly,* with the pudding. It was so hard and firm.* Christmas holly was stuck into the top.

"Oh, a wonderful pudding!" said Bob Cratchit.

He thought it was the greatest success achieved* by Mrs. Cratchit since their marriage.* Mrs. Cratchit said that now that she was no longer nervous, she could tell them how worried she had been. Everybody had something to say about it, but nobody said or thought it was at all a small pudding for a large family. Any Cratchit would have blushed* to hint* at such a thing.

At last the dinner was all done, the cloth was cleared, the fireplace swept, and the fire was lit again. The gin and lemon juice in the jug was tasted, and it was perfect. Apples and oranges were put upon the table, and many chestnuts were put on the fire. Then all the Cratchit family went around the fireplace. Bob Cratchit's elbow* was next to the family's fancy glass cups. One of them was a little broken.

These held the hot stuff* from the jug,

---

imagine 상상하다, 마음에 그리다 **proudly** 의기양양하게 **firm** 단단한, 견고한 **achieve** 이루다, 달성하다 **marriage** 결혼, 혼인 **blush** 얼굴을 붉히다 **hint** 넌지시 비추다, 암시하다 **elbow** 팔꿈치 **stuff** 물질, 성분

however, as well as golden cups would have done. Bob served it out with a huge smile while the chestnuts on the fire cracked[*] noisily.[*]

"A merry Christmas to us all, my dears," said Bob. "God bless us!"

All the family repeated it.

"God bless us every one!" said Tiny Tim, the last of all.

He sat very close to his father's side on his little stool. Bob held his weak little hand in his, as if he loved the child. He wished to keep him by his side and feared that he might lose him.

"Spirit, tell me if Tiny Tim will live," said Scrooge, with an interest he had never felt before.

"I see an empty seat in the corner and a crutch without an owner," replied the Spirit. "If these shadows remain unchanged by the Future, the child will die."

"No, no," said Scrooge. "Oh, no, kind Spirit! Say it's not true!"

"If these shadows remain unchanged by the Future, he will not see another Christmas," said the Spirit. "What then? If he is likely to* die, he had better do it. That way the population will decrease.* There are too many people, right?"

Scrooge hung his head to hear his own words said by the Spirit. He was filled with regret.

"If you are just a man, how can you choose who the extra* person is, and where he is?" said the Spirit. "Will you decide what men shall live and what men shall die? Are you any better than this poor man's child or people like him? To God,

---

crack 우지끈 하며 깨지다 **noisily** 요란하게, 소란스럽게 **be likely to** ~할 것 같다 **decrease** 줄다, 감소하다 **extra** 여분의, 추가의

you are also like the insect* on a leaf."

Scrooge bent before the Spirit's words, and shaking, he looked down at the ground. But he raised his eyes swiftly,* when he heard his own name.

"Mr. Scrooge!" said Bob. "I'll toast* to you Mr. Scrooge, who gave us money for this feast*!"

"Indeed!" cried Mrs. Cratchit, turning red. "I wish I had him here. I'd show him what I really think about him! I hope he'd be ready!"

"My dear," said Bob. "Don't say that in front of the children on Christmas Day."

"Christmas Day is the only day that one drinks to the health of such a terrible, hard, unfeeling* man as Mr. Scrooge," said Mrs. Cratchit. "You know he is, Bob! Nobody knows it better than you do, poor man!"

"My dear, it's Christmas Day," said Bob.

"I'll drink to his health for you, or because it's Christmas, but not for his," said Mrs. Cratchit. "Long life to him! A merry Christmas and a happy New Year! He'll be very merry and very happy. I have no doubt!"

The children drank the toast after her. It was the first thing they did that day that they didn't like. Tiny Tim drank it last of all, but he didn't like it at all. Scrooge was a monster* to the family. Talking about him put a dark shadow, which stayed there for a full five minutes, over the party.

After it had passed away, they were ten times merrier than before because they didn't have to talk about Scrooge again. Bob Cratchit told them how he found a job for Master Peter. The two young

insect 벌레, 곤충 **swiftly** 신속히, 빨리 **toast** 건배하다, 축배하다 **feast** 잔치, 진수성찬 **unfeeling** 무정한, 잔혹한 **monster** 괴물, 도깨비

Cratchits laughed tremendously* at the idea of Peter's being a man of business. Peter himself looked thoughtfully* at the fire, trying to decide how he would spend his money.

Martha, who was a poor apprentice, then told them what kind of work she had to do and how many hours she worked. She wanted to sleep all day the next day because it was a holiday. Also, she talked about how she had seen a countess* and a lord* some days before. She said that the lord "was about as tall as Peter." All this time, the chestnuts and the jug went around and around. They sang a song about a lost child traveling in the snow. Tiny Tim sang with a beautiful little voice.

There was nothing rich about them. They were not a handsome family. They were not well dressed. Their shoes were wet, their clothes were old, and Peter was often in trouble.* But they were happy, grateful,* pleased with one another, and happier at Christmas time. When they faded, they looked even happier after the Spirit sprinkled magic on them. Scrooge watched them, and especially Tiny Tim, until the end.

By this time, it was getting dark and snowing pretty heavily. As Scrooge and the Spirit walked along the streets, the brightness of the roaring fires in kitchens, living rooms, and all sorts of rooms, was wonderful. The light showed the preparations for* a comfortable dinner with hot plates baking in front of the fire.

The windows had deep red curtains ready to be closed to keep out the cold and darkness. All the children of the house

tremendously 굉장히, 몹시 **thoughtfully** 생각을 깊게 하여, 생각에 잠겨 **countess** 백작 부인 **lord** 영주 **be in trouble** 곤란한 처지에 있다 **grateful** 고맙게 여기는, 감사하는 **preparations for** ~에 대한 준비

were running out into the snow to meet their married sisters, brothers, cousins, uncles, aunts, and be the first to greet them.

At another house were the shadows of a different group. There was a group of handsome girls, all in hoods* and fur boots, and all talking at once.* They looked beautiful and glowing! Any single* man who saw them would fall in love with them!

Because there were so many people visiting other people, it was hard to believe that there were people in the houses waiting for them to come! The Spirit was so happy! He opened its hands and gave blessings and happiness to everyone! The man who lit the lamps at night, and who was dressed to spend the evening somewhere, laughed loudly as the Spirit passed!

And now, without a warning from the Spirit, they stood at an empty place. There were large pieces of stone as though giants were buried* there. Water was frozen in strange patterns. Nothing grew but moss* and grass. Down in the west, the setting sun looked fiery* red. It was sinking* lower, lower, lower, and was lost in the thick gloom of the darkest night.

"What place is this?" asked Scrooge.

"A place where miners* who work deep underearth live," replied the Spirit. "But they know me. See!"

A light shone from the window of a hut,* and swiftly they ran toward it. Passing through the wall of mud and stone, they found a cheerful company* sitting around a glowing fire. An old, old

hood 두건 **at once** 한꺼번에, 동시에 **single** 혼자의, 독신의 **bury** 묻다, 매장하다 **moss** 이끼 **fiery** 타는 듯한 **sink** 지다, 가라앉다 **miner** 광부 **hut** 오두막집 **company** 동료, 일행

man and woman, with their children and their children's children, and even their children, were all dressed in their holiday clothes.

The old man, in a voice that usually was never louder than the sound of the wind, was singing them a Christmas song. Sometimes they all joined in the chorus.* The old man enjoyed when the others sang with him, and he sang even louder.

The Spirit did not wait here a long time but asked Scrooge to hold its robe. Where would they go? Not to sea? They flew to the sea. To Scrooge's horror, looking back, he saw the last of the land and scary* rocks behind them. He could not hear because of the loud sound of water crashing against the rocks.

Built on those scary rocks, far from shore, where the water was wild, there was a single lighthouse.* Pieces of seaweed* stuck to the bottom of it and large sea birds flew around it.

But even here, two men who watched the light had made a fire. Through the hole in the thick stone wall, it gave a ray of brightness on the awful sea. Joining their rough hands over the rough table at which they sat, they wished each other a merry Christmas. One of them, the older, with his face all damaged* and scarred,* starting singing a song that was like a strong wind.

Again the Spirit flew on, above the black and moving sea, on and on, until they found a ship. They stood beside the captain.* The men who worked on the ship looked like dark, ghostly figures. Yet every man among them hummed* a Christmas song or had a Christmas

---

chorus 합창 **scary** 무서운, 두려운 **lighthouse** 등대 **seaweed** 해초, 해조 **damage** 손해를 입히다 **scar** 흉터를 남기다 **captain** 선장 **hum** 콧노래를 부르다

thought.

And every man on board* had had a kind thing to say to the other men. Every man had joined the party and celebrations.* Every man had remembered those whom he cared for at a distance. Every man knew that they were happy to remember him.

It was a great surprise to Scrooge, who listened to the sound of the wind. He was thinking how lonely it would be to sail over the dark, unknown ocean. The ocean had secrets as old as death. It was a great surprise to Scrooge to hear a laugh as he was thinking. It was a much greater surprise to Scrooge to recognize it as his own nephew's. He was now in a bright, dry, shining room. The Spirit was standing, smiling by his side, and looking at that same nephew happily!

"Ha, ha!" laughed Scrooge's nephew.

"Ha, ha, ha!"

It is fair to say that nothing is as good as laughter and jokes. When Scrooge's nephew laughed, by holding his sides, rolling his head, and changing his face, Scrooge's niece,* by marriage, laughed as well. All of their friends also laughed. "Ha, ha! Ha, ha, ha, ha!"

"He said that Christmas was a humbug!" cried Scrooge's nephew. "He believed it too!"

"More shame for him, Fred!" said Scrooge's niece. Bless those women. They always say what they think. They are always honest.

She was very pretty. She had a surprised-looking, gorgeous* face and a little mouth that made you want to kiss on. She had the sunniest pair of eyes! She

on board 배에 타고 **celebration** 축하, 의식 **niece** 조카딸, 조카며느리
gorgeous 찬란한, 눈부신

was very beautiful, but she was also very comfortable and easy to talk to.

"He's a funny old man," said Scrooge's nephew. "That's the truth. He could be more pleasant. However, he only punishes* himself, and I have nothing to say against him."

"I'm sure he is very rich, Fred," said Scrooge's niece. "At least you always tell me so."

"What of that, my dear?" said Scrooge's nephew. "His money is of no use* to him. He doesn't do any good with it. He doesn't make himself comfortable with it. He doesn't have anyone to share it with."

"I have no patience* with him," said Scrooge's niece. Scrooge's niece's sisters, and all the other ladies, had the same opinion.

"Oh, I have!" said Scrooge's nephew. "I am sorry for him. I couldn't be angry with him however hard I tried. He is the one who suffers. He decides to dislike* us, and he doesn't eat dinner with us. It doesn't hurt us. He's the one that loses dinner."

"Indeed, I think he loses a very good dinner," said Scrooge's niece. Everybody else said the same. They had just had dinner and the dessert was on the table. They were gathered around the fire by lamplight.*

"Well, I'm very glad to hear it," said Scrooge's nephew. "Because I don't have great faith in these young housekeepers.* What do you say, Topper?"

Topper was clearly interested in one of Scrooge's niece's sisters, because he half-heartedly* answered that a single man had no idea of those things. Scrooge's niece's

punish 벌하다, 응징하다 **of no use** 소용없는 **patience** 참을성, 인내 **dislike** 싫어하다, 좋아하지 않다 **lamplight** 등불, 등화 **housekeeper** 가정부 **half-heartedly** 건성으로

sister blushed.

"Do go on, Fred," said Scrooge's niece, clapping her hands. "He never finishes what he begins to say! He is such a ridiculous man!"

Scrooge's nephew laughed again, as it was impossible not to. The sister tried not to laugh, but she also began to laugh.

"I was only going to say that because he dislikes us and does not make merry with us, he loses some pleasant moments. I am sure we are more pleasant companions* than the things which he might find in his old office or dusty* rooms. I mean to give him the same chance every year, whether he likes it or not, for I pity him. He may hate Christmas till he dies, but he must like it a little better if I go there every year, in a good mood.* Who knows? Maybe he will feel good and give his clerk a Christmas present. I think I may have changed his mind yesterday."

They all laughed at the idea of changing Scrooge's mind. Scrooge's nephew was kind, so he didn't care what they laughed at. He encouraged them to keep laughing. He passed them the bottle.

After tea, they sang a few songs. They were a musical* family and knew what they were good at. Topper could sing very deeply and did not feel any stress.* Scrooge's niece played the harp well. She played a very simple song that Scrooge's sister used to sing.

When this song started, all the things that the Spirit had shown him, came upon his mind. He softened* more and more. He thought that if he could have listened to it often, years ago, he might have

---

companion 동료, 친구 **dusty** 먼지투성이의 **in a good mood** 기분이 좋은
musical 음악적인 **stress** 압박감, 스트레스 **soften** 누그러지다

become kinder and happier.

But they didn't sing the whole evening. After a while, they played cards, for it is good to be children sometimes, and never better than at Christmas. Then, they played blind man's buff.* Topper did not really close his eyes. Scrooge's nephew had chosen this game to give Topper a chance to chase* his wife's sister. He clumsily* followed the sister everywhere. He wouldn't catch anybody else.

She often cried out that it wasn't fair, and it really was not. But when at last, he caught her, though she kept running from him, he got her into a corner, and she could not escape.

He behaved* as if he didn't know who she was. With his eyes closed, he kept touching her face and body. Finally he stopped when he put a ring on her finger and necklace* around her neck! No doubt she told him her opinion of it when they hid together behind the curtains.

Scrooge's niece did not play blind man's buff but was sitting comfortably with a large chair and a footstool* in a comfortable corner. The Spirit and Scrooge were close behind her. But she joined in the games later, and said a million* praises about her husband.

Likewise,* at the game of how, when, and where, she was also very good. To the secret joy of Scrooge's nephew, she was much better than her sisters. There might have been twenty people there, young and old, but they all played, and so did Scrooge.

He was so interested by the games that he completely* forgot that his voice made

---

blind man's buff 까막잡기 **chase** 뒤쫓다, 추구하다 **clumsily** 어색하게, 꼴사납게 **behave** 행동하다 **necklace** 목걸이 **footstool** 휴대용 발판 **million** 백만의 **likewise** 마찬가지로, 또한 **completely** 완전히, 완벽하게

no sound in their ears. He sometimes yelled* his guess* quite loudly, and very often guessed quite right, too. Scrooge was actually* very smart.

The Spirit was greatly pleased to see him playing and looked at him with a smile. He begged, like a boy, the Spirit to let him stay until the guests* departed.* But the Spirit said he could not do that.

"Here is a new game," said Scrooge. "One half hour, Spirit, only one!"

It was a game called Yes and No in something that Scrooge's nephew had to think of, and the rest must find out what. He answered their questions only with a yes or no. The first questions he heard revealed* that he was thinking of an animal, a live animal, an angry animal, a wild animal. It was an animal that growled and grunted* sometimes. It even talked sometimes! It lived in London and walked around the streets.

But it was not in a show! Nobody walked with it, and it didn't live in a zoo. It was never killed in a market and was not a horse, or an ass, or a cow, or a bull, or a tiger, or a dog, or a pig, or a cat, or a bear. At every new question that was asked to him, this nephew burst into* a new roar of laughter. He laughed so much that he had to stand up and stamp his feet* on the ground. At last the sister also began to laugh like crazy.

"I have found it out!" she cried. "I know what it is, Fred! I know what it is!"

"What is it?" cried Fred.

"It's your Uncle Scro-o-o-o-oge!"

It certainly* was. Everyone felt pleased at this answer and began to laugh, too.

yell 큰 소리를 지르다 **guess** 추측, 짐작 **actually** 실지로, 실제로 **guest** 손님, 내빈 **depart** 출발하다, 떠나다 **reveal** 드러내다 **grunt** 툴툴거리다, 불평하다 **burst into** 갑자기 ~하다 **stamp one's feet** 발을 동동 구르다 **certainly** 확실히, 틀림없이

"He has given us lots of entertainment,*" said Scrooge's nephew. "It would be ungrateful* not to drink to his health. Everyone pick up a glass of red wine and get ready! I say, 'Bless you, Uncle Scrooge!'"

"To Uncle Scrooge!" they cried.

"A merry Christmas and a happy New Year to the old man, whatever* he is!" said Scrooge's nephew. "He wouldn't take it from me, but may he have it anyway,* Uncle Scrooge!"

Scrooge suddenly became so happy and touched* that he would have thanked his nephew, if the Spirit had given him time. But the whole scene* changed after the breath of the last word spoken by his nephew. He and the Spirit were again on their travels.

Much they saw, and far they went, and many homes they visited, but always with a happy end. The Spirit stood beside sickbeds,* and the patients were cheerful. On foreign lands, people made themselves at home. Even struggling* men were patient as they wished for greater things.

Even the poor felt rich. In the homeless* shelter,* hospital, and jail,* and in every sad place where the people had not closed their door to Christmas, did it drop. It blessed them all. It was a long night, if it were only one night. But Scrooge had his doubts about this, because the Christmas holidays all seemed to pass at the same time.

It was strange, too, that while Scrooge looked the same, the Spirit grew older, clearly older. Scrooge had seen this

entertainment 오락, 기분 전환 **ungrateful** 은혜를 모르는, 배은망덕의 **whatever** 무엇이든지 **anyway** 어쨌든, 아무튼 **touched** 감동받은 **scene** 장면 **sickbed** 병상 **struggling** 발버둥 치는, 분투하는 **the homeless** 집 없는 사람들, 노숙자 **shelter** 보호소, 피난처 **jail** 교도소, 감옥

change, but never spoke of it until they left a children's party. Then, when looking at the Spirit as they stood together in an open place, he saw that its hair was gray.

"Are spirits' lives so short?" asked Scrooge.

"My life upon this earth, is very brief," replied the Spirit. "It ends tonight."

"Tonight!" cried Scrooge.

"Tonight at midnight," said the Spirit. "Listen! The time is coming soon."

The clock was saying three quarters past eleven at that moment.

"I don't know if I am supposed to ask this," said Scrooge, looking closely at the Spirit's robe. "But I see something strange that is not a part of you and under your robe. Is it a foot or a claw*?"

"It might be a claw, for there is skin* on it," replied the Spirit sorrowfully.* "Look here."

From the inside of its robe, two children came out. They looked poor, dirty, sick, and sad. They knelt down* at its feet and grabbed the outside of its robe.

"Oh, Man!" exclaimed the Spirit. "Look here. Look, look, down here!"

They were a boy and girl. They were yellow, thin, ugly, frowning,* and like wolves. But they were bowing their heads quietly as they begged. At their age, they should have looked young, happy, and cheerful, but something made them look very old and tired. They should have looked like angels, but instead they looked like devils.* There were no monsters or demons* as frightening* as these children.

Scrooge backed away, disgusted.* He tried to think of something nice to say

claw 갈고리 발톱 **skin** 가죽, 껍질 **sorrowfully** 구슬프게 **kneel down** 꿇어앉다 **frowning** 찌푸린 얼굴의, 험상궂은 표정의 **devil** 악마, 악귀 **demon** 악마, 마귀 **frightening** 깜짝 놀라게 하는, 겁을 주는 **disgusted** 메스꺼운, 역겨운

about the children. He didn't want to say something bad, but he could not lie. The words would not come out of his mouth.

"Spirit!" said Scrooge. "Are they yours?"

"They are Man's," said the Spirit, looking down at them. "And they hug me, begging for me to help their fathers. This boy is Ignorance.* This girl is Want.* You should be scared of both of them. But most of all* fear this boy. In his face, I see Doom.* I see the end of the world. Change it!"

"Do they have no house or food?" asked Scrooge.

"Are there no prisons?" said the Spirit, repeating Scrooge's past words. "Are there no workhouses?"

The bell struck twelve.

Scrooge looked around him for the Spirit, but he did not see it. As the last bell stopped ringing, he remembered what

Jacob Marley had told him. He looked up. He saw a serious,* quiet Spirit wearing a long robe and a hood walking toward him, out of the mist.

---

ignorance 무지 **want** 곤궁, 빈곤 **most of all** 무엇보다도 **doom** 파멸, 운명 **serious** 엄숙한, 진지한

Chapter 04

The Last of the Three Spirits

마지막으로 스크루지에게 미래의 크리스마스 유령이 찾아온다.
유령은 스크루지에게 비참하게 홀로 죽은 사람의 모습을 보여 주고
그를 무덤으로 이끌어 그 죽은 사람이 스크루지임을 깨닫게 해 준다.
놀란 스크루지는 자신의 미래를 바꿀 기회를 달라고 간청한다.

The Spirit slowly, silently approached. When the Spirit came near him, Scrooge bent down on his knee. It was wearing a deep black robe, which covered its head, its face, and its body. The only part of its body that he could see was one hand. If he could not have seen the hand, he would not have been able to see the Spirit in the dark night.

Scrooge felt that it was tall and noble when it came beside him, and its mysterious* presence filled him with fear. He knew no more, for the Spirit neither spoke nor moved.

"Am I in the presence of* the Spirit of Christmas Future?" asked Scrooge.

The Spirit did not answer but pointed at something with its hand.

"You are about to show me shadows of the things that have not happened, but will happen in the future?" Scrooge asked. "Is that so, Spirit?"

The hood of its robe moved a little as if the Spirit had turned its head. That was the only answer he received.* Although he had become used to ghosts by now,* Scrooge

---

mysterious 신비한, 불가사의한 **in the presence of** ~의 면전에서
receive 받다, 얻다 **by now** 지금쯤은

feared the silent shape so much that his legs shook beneath him. He realized that he could hardly* stand when he tried to follow it. The Spirit stopped a moment, watching him, and waited.

But this made Scrooge feel worse. It filled him with horror. He did not want to think that behind the hood there were ghostly eyes watching him carefully. Meanwhile, he could only see one hand.

"Spirit of the Future!" he exclaimed. "I fear you more than any Spirit I have seen. But, as I know you want to help me and change me into a better man, I will thank you. Will you not speak to me?"

It gave him no reply. The hand was pointed straight in front of them.

"Lead on*!" said Scrooge. "Lead on! The night is going quickly, and it is precious* time to me, I know. Lead on, Spirit!"

The Spirit began walking away quietly.

Scrooge followed in the shadow of its robe, which seemed to carry him.

They suddenly entered a city. It was surprising! It seemed to come from nowhere*! But there they were, in the heart of* it. Men ran up and down with coins ringing in their pockets, talked in groups, and looked at their watches. They were the kind of men that Scrooge had seen often.

The Spirit stopped beside one little group of businessmen. Seeing that the hand was pointed at them, Scrooge approached to listen to their talk.

"No, I don't know much about it, anyway," said a great fat man with a tremendous chin. "I only know he's dead."

"When did he die?" asked another.

"Last night, I believe," said the fat man.

---

hardly 거의 ~ 않는 **lead on** (계속하여) 안내하다 **precious** 귀중한, 값비싼
nowhere 어디인지 모르는 곳, 미지의 장소 **in the heart of** ~의 한복판에

"Why, what was the matter with him?" asked a third, who was smoking. "I thought he'd never die."

"God knows," said the fat man with a yawn.*

"What has he done with his money?" asked a red-faced gentleman with a huge pimple* on his nose that shook when he talked.

"I haven't heard," said the fat man, yawning again. "He left it to his company, perhaps. He hasn't left it to me. That's all I know."

The men all laughed at this joke.

"It's likely to be a very cheap funeral," said the fat man. "I don't know of anybody who will go to it. Suppose we make a party and volunteer*?"

"I don't mind going if we get lunch," said the gentleman with the pimple on his nose. "But I must be fed."

There was another laugh.

"Well, I have no reason to go," said the fat man. "I never wear black gloves, and I never eat lunch. But I'll go if anybody else will. When I think of it, I might have been his best friend. We did talk a little. Bye, bye!"

Speakers and listeners walked away and mixed with other groups. Scrooge knew the men and looked toward the Spirit for an explanation. The Spirit floated into a street. Its finger pointed to two people who were meeting. Scrooge listened again, thinking that the explanation might be here.

He knew these men, also, perfectly. They were men of business, very rich, and of great importance.* He always tried to make them like him, because it was good

---

yawn 하품 **pimple** 뾰루지 **volunteer** 지원자, 자원 봉사자 **of great importance** 아주 중요한

for business.

"How are you?" said one.

"How are you?" said the other.

"Well!" said the first. "Old Scratch* has finally died, huh?"

"So I am told," said the second. "Cold, isn't it?"

"It's normal for Christmas time," said the first. "You're not a skater,* I suppose?"

"No, no," said the second. "I don't skate. Good morning!"

There was not another word. That was their meeting, their talk, and their parting.

Scrooge was at first surprised that the Spirit would make him listen to such unimportant* conversations.* But he also thought that the Spirit must have some hidden reason for showing him. He thought about what that reason might be. They could not be talking about Jacob, because this was the future.

He could not think of anyone he knew that they might be talking about. But he didn't doubt that whoever they were talking about had something to teach him. So he decided to listen carefully to everything.

He looked around for his own image, but another man stood in his usual corner. Though the clock pointed to his usual* time of day for being there, he did not see himself. It gave him little surprise, however. He had been deciding to change his life, and thought and hoped that he was now watching what happened after those changes.

Quiet and dark, beside him stood the Spirit, with its pointing hand. When he stopped thinking about things, he watched the Spirit again. He imagined its eyes on

---

Old Scratch 악마 **skater** 스케이트를 타는 사람 **unimportant** 중요하지 않은, 하찮은 **conversation** 대화 **usual** 보통의, 평상시의

him again. It made him shake and feel very cold.

They left the busy scene and went into a little known part of the town where Scrooge had never been before. He recognized that it was not a good part of town. The roads were dangerous and narrow. The shops and houses looked poor, and the people were half-naked, drunken, and ugly. Alleys* were filled with dirt. It smelled like crime* and pain.

They finally arrived at a shop where iron, old rags,* bottles, bones, and grease* were bought. On the floor inside, were piles of rusty* keys, nails,* chains, hinges, files,* scales,* weights,* and iron of all kinds. Secrets that were better not known were hidden under the bones, iron, and grease.

Sitting among the products* in the store, by a stove made of old bricks, was a gray-haired* man, nearly seventy years of age. Even though it was cold, he only wore rags. He smoked a pipe and relaxed.

Scrooge and the Spirit saw this man just as a woman with a heavy package walked into the shop. But she had just entered, when another woman, also with a package, came in, too. She was closely followed by a man in faded black. As they recognized one another, they all looked surprised. After a few moments of astonishment, all three burst into laughter.

"Let the cleaning woman be the first!" cried the woman who had entered first. "Let the laundress* be the second, and let the undertaker's man be the third. Look here, old Joe! We all met one another!"

"You couldn't have met in a better

alley 샛길, 골목길 **crime** 죄, 범죄 **rag** 넝마 **grease** 그리스, 유지 **rusty** 녹슨 **nail** 못, 징 **file** 철끈 **scale** 저울 **weight** 저울추 **product** 생산품, 제품 **gray-haired** 백발의 **laundress** (여자) 세탁부

place," said old Joe, removing* his pipe from his mouth. "Come into the living room. You are not strangers.* I'll close the shop. Ah! Both my bones and these doors make a lot of noise when they move! Ha, ha! We're all well matched.* Come into the living room. Come into the living room."

The living room was a small space behind some rags. The old man made a fire and lit a lamp with his pipe. He put it back in his mouth and resumed smoking.

While he did this, the woman who had already spoken threw her package on the floor and sat down on a stool. She crossed her elbows on her knees. She looked boldly* at the other two.

"Every person should take care of themselves, Mrs. Dilber," said the woman. "He always did."

"That's true, indeed!" said the laundress.

"Why then, don't stare at me like you're

afraid," said the woman. "We're not going to tell the police about one another, I suppose?"

"No, indeed!" said Mrs. Dilber and the man together. "We should hope not."

"Very well, then!" cried the woman. "That's enough. We all agree that he's dead and doesn't need these things anymore."

"That's right," said Mrs. Dilber, laughing.

"If he wanted to keep them after he was dead, why wasn't he kinder in his lifetime*?" said the woman. "If he had been, he'd have had somebody to look after him when he was dying, instead of dying alone."

"It's the truest word that ever was spoken," said Mrs. Dilber.

"I wish something worse happened to

remove 치우다, 제거하다 **stranger** 낯선 사람 **match** 조화되다, 어울리다
boldly 거만하게, 대담하게 **in one's lifetime** 살면서, ~의 생애에서

him," said the woman. "Something worse will happen. Open that package of stuff I took from his house, old Joe, and let me know how much it is. Be honest. I'm not afraid to be the first, nor afraid for them to see it. We all know that we took stuff from his house, I believe. It's not bad. Open the package, Joe."

But her friends didn't want her to be first. The man in faded black opened his package first. It wasn't that much. There was a stamp or two, a pencil case, a pair of sleeve-buttons, and a brooch.* Nothing looked expensive. They were looked over* a few times and given a price by old Joe. He wrote the prices on the wall with chalk and added them all together.

"That's your total," said Joe. "I can't give you any more than this. Who's next?"

Mrs. Dilber was next. She had sheets* and towels, some clothing, two old silver teaspoons, and a few boots. Her total was stated on the wall in the same way.

"I always give too much to ladies," said old Joe. "It's a weakness* of mine, and that's the way I ruin* myself. That's your total. If you asked me for another penny, I wouldn't give it to you."

"And now open my package, Joe," said the first woman.

Joe went down on his knees to make it easier to open it. He pulled out a heavy roll of some dark stuff.

"What do you call this?" said Joe. "Bed curtains!"

"Ah!" said the woman, laughing and leaning forward* on her crossed arms. "Bed curtains!"

"You don't mean to say you took them down with him lying dead there?" asked

brooch 브로치 **look over** 조사하다, 자세히 살펴보다 **sheet** 침대보
weakness 약점 **ruin** 파멸시키다 **forward** 앞으로

Joe.

"Yes, I do," replied the woman. "Why not?"

"You were born to make your fortune," said Joe. "You'll certainly do it."

"I definitely don't feel bad taking from a man like him," said the woman coolly.* "Don't drop that oil upon the blankets, now."

"His blankets?" asked Joe.

"Whose else's do you think?" said the woman. "He's dead. Who cares if he's cold?"

"I hope he didn't die of some illness* that you could catch, eh?" said old Joe, stopping in his work and looking up.

"You don't need to be afraid of that," said the woman. "I don't like him enough to stay around his body long enough to catch something. Ah! You can look at that shirt till your eyes hurt, but there are no holes. It's the best he had and an expensive one too. They'd have wasted it, if it hadn't been for me."

"What do you mean, it would have been wasted?" asked old Joe.

"Putting it on him to be buried in," replied the woman with a laugh. "Somebody was fool enough to do it, but I took it off again. It looks nice, but nothing would make him look handsome."

Scrooge listened to this talk in horror. They sat grouped around their stolen* stuff. In the little light given by the old man's lamp, Scrooge watched them with disgust.* He thought they were like demons because they were selling a dead man's things.

"Ha, ha!" laughed the laundress when old Joe gave them their money. "This is the

coolly 서늘하게, 냉담하게　**illness** 병　**stolen** 훔친　**with disgust** 혐오스러움을 느끼며

end of it, you see! He frightened everyone away* from him when he was alive! But now that he's dead, we can take his stuff!"

"Spirit!" said Scrooge, shaking from head to foot. "I see, I see. The case of this unhappy man might be my own. My life is going this way. Heaven, what is this?"

He jumped back in terror, for the scene had changed. Now he almost touched a bed, a bare bed with no curtains. Beneath the sheet was something covered up. The room was very dark. It was too dark to see clearly.

Yet, Scrooge looked around anyway, anxious to* know what kind of room it was. A pale light, rising from the air outside, fell straight upon the bed. On this bed with everything stolen, with no one watching it, no one caring for it, was the body of this man.

Scrooge looked at the Spirit. Its steady*

hand was pointed to the head. If Scrooge had moved the cover over its head just a little bit, he could have seen the man's face. He thought of it, felt how easy it would be to do, and longed to* do it. Yet, he had no power to move anything.

Oh, cold, dreadful Death, you are king here! If someone is loved or respected,* Death does not make him look bad or frightening. If he is brave, noble, and kind, his death will be different! People will think about his death differently!

No voice cried for this man, and yet Scrooge felt like* crying for this man. He thought, if this man could be alive again, what he would think. Would he think about greed and business? They have not helped this man!

---

frighten away 위협하여 몰아내다 **anxious to** ~을 열망하여, 몹시 ~하고 싶어 하는 **steady** 흔들리지 않는, 확고부동한 **long to** ~을 열망하다, 갈망하다 **respect** 존경하다 **feel like -ing** ~하고 싶다

He lay, in the dark empty house, with not a man, a woman, or a child to remember him. Scrooge tried to think of something kind to say about the man who was alone and dead. A cat was scratching at the door, and there was a sound of rats coming from beneath the floor. Scrooge did not want to think about why they wanted to enter the room.

"Spirit!" he said. "This is a fearful* place. When we leave, I will not forget its lesson. Trust me. Let's go!"

Still the Spirit pointed with an unmoved finger to the head.

"I understand you," said Scrooge. "I would look, if I could. But I don't have the power, Spirit. I don't have the power."

Again it seemed to look at him.

"If there is any person in the town who feels sadness caused by this man's death, show that person to me, Spirit," said

Scrooge, feeling great pain. "I beg you!"

The Spirit opened his dark robe, like wings. When he closed his arms, he revealed* a room in daylight,* where a mother and her children were.

She was expecting someone with anxious eagerness.* She walked up and down the room. She jumped at every sound and looked out from the window. She stared at the clock. She tried to sew,* but she could not focus.* She was annoyed by the voices of the children in their play.

Finally, the long expected knock was heard. She hurried to the door and met her husband, a man whose face looked tired and sad, though he was young. In his eyes, Scrooge thought he could see a sparkle* of delight that he tried to hide.

fearful 무시무시한, 두려운 **reveal** 드러내다 **daylight** 일광, 빛 **with eagerness** 열망하여 **sew** 바느질하다, 꿰매다 **focus** 집중하다, 초점을 맞추다 **sparkle** 불꽃, 광채

He sat down to the dinner that had been waiting for him by the fire. When she finally asked him what news he had, he looked embarrassed.

"Is it good?" she asked. "Or bad?"

"Bad," he replied.

"We are quite ruined*?" she asked.

"No," he said. "There is hope yet, Caroline."

"If he changes his mind, there is!" she said. "But it's impossible."

"He can't change his mind," said her husband. "He is dead."

She was a calm and patient creature, but she was thankful in her soul* to hear this news. She said thank you with clasped hands. She said sorry the next moment. But the first thing she felt was thankful.

"I didn't believe that drunken woman the other night when she told me," he said. "But I checked* today. It was true. He was not only very ill, but dying, then."

"Now who do we owe* money to?" she asked.

"I don't know," he said. "But before that time, we shall be ready with the money. Even if we are not, the new person will be kinder than he was. We may sleep tonight with light hearts, Caroline!"

Yes. Their hearts were lighter. The children's faces were brighter! The house became happier because this man died! The only feeling that the Spirit could show him, caused by that man's death, was one of pleasure.

"Let me see someone feel sad about this death," said Scrooge. "Or that dark bedroom, Spirit, which we left just now, will be forever in my memory."

The Spirit led him through several

ruined 몰락한, 파산한 **soul** 영혼, 정신 **check** 조사하다, 점검하다 **owe** 빚지고 있다, 지불할 의무가 있다

streets familiar to his feet. And as they went along, Scrooge looked here and there to find himself, but he was nowhere. They entered poor Bob Cratchit's house, the house he had visited before, and found the mother and the children sitting around the fire.

It was quiet. It was very quiet. The noisy little Cratchits were not moving in the one corner. They sat looking up at Peter, who had a book in front of him. The mother and her daughters were busy sewing. But surely they were very quiet!

"And He took a child, and put him down in the middle of them," said Peter.

Where had Scrooge heard those words? He had not dreamed them. The boy must have read them out as he and the Spirit entered the house. Why did he not continue?

The mother laid her work on the table

and put her hands up to her face.

"The color hurts my eyes," she said.

The color? Ah, where was Tiny Tim?

"They're better now again," said Cratchit's wife. "That color isn't good to look at by candlelight. Where is your father? It must be almost time for him to come home."

"It's late," replied Peter, closing his book. "But I think he has walked a little slower than he used to these last few evenings, Mother."

They were very quiet again.

"I remember he used to walk with Tiny Tim on his shoulder, very quickly," she said and tried to sound cheerful.

"And so do I," cried Peter. "Often."

"And so do I," exclaimed another. So did all.

"But he was very light to carry," she said, focusing on her work. "And his father loved him, so it was no trouble. And there is your father at the door!"

She ran out to meet him, and little Bob in his blanket, came inside. His tea was ready for him on the stove, and they all tried to give it to him. Then the two young Cratchits got on his knees and laid a little cheek against his face.

Bob was very cheerful with them and spoke pleasantly to all the family. He looked at the work on the table and praised the design and speed of Mrs. Cratchit and the girls. They would be finished long before Sunday, he said.

"Sunday!" said his wife. "You went today, then, Robert?"

"Yes, my dear," replied Bob. "I wish you could have gone. It would have been good for you to see how green a place it is. But you'll see it often. I promised him that I would walk there on Sunday. My little,

little child!" cried Bob. "My little child!"

He began weeping immediately. He couldn't help it. He left the room and went into the room upstairs, which was lighted cheerfully and hung with Christmas decorations. There was a chair sitting close beside the child, and there were signs of someone having been there, lately. Poor Bob sat down in it. After he stopped crying, he felt a little comforted and went downstairs again.

They sat around the fire and talked, the girls and mother working still. Bob told them about the amazing kindness of Mr. Scrooge's nephew, whom he had only met once.

According to* Bob, when meeting him in the street that day and seeing that Bob looked a little sad, Mr. Scrooge's nephew

according to ~에 의하면

asked what had happened to upset him.

"On which, for he is the kindest gentleman you've ever heard, I told him," said Bob. "'I am heartily* sorry for it, Mr. Cratchit, and heartily sorry for your good wife,' he said. By the way, how he ever knew that, I don't know."

"Knew what, my dear?" asked Mrs. Cratchit.

"Why, that you were a good wife," replied Bob.

"Everybody knows that!" said Peter.

"That's true, my boy!" cried Bob. "I hope they do. 'Truly sorry for your good wife. If I can help you in any way, come visit me,' he said. He was quite delightful. It really seemed as if he had known our Tiny Tim and felt sad with us."

"I'm sure he's a good soul!" said Mrs. Cratchit.

"You would be surer of it, my dear, if

you saw and spoke to him," said Bob. "I won't be surprised even if he helps us find Peter a better job."

"Did you hear that, Peter?" said Mrs. Cratchit.

"And then, Peter will meet a nice girl," cried one of the girls. "And then he will start saving money so that they can get married."

"Oh, be quiet!" said Peter, smiling.

"It could happen," said Bob. "It could happen in the future. We can think about that later, my dear. But no matter where we go or what we do, I am sure that none of us will forget poor Tiny Tim. He is the first one of us to leave this world."

"Never, Father!" they all cried.

"And I know," said Bob. "I know, my dears, that when we remember how

---

heartily 진심으로

patient and how calm he was, although he was a little child, we shall not argue* among ourselves."

"No, never, Father!" they all cried again.

"I am very happy," said Bob. "I am very happy!"

Mrs. Cratchit kissed him, his daughters kissed him, the two young Cratchits kissed him, and Peter and he shook hands. Tiny Tim, there was something special and beautiful about you!

"Spirit, something tells me that you will leave soon," said Scrooge. "I know it, but I don't know how. Tell me who the dead man was."

The Spirit of Christmas led him to a different time and place. He moved quickly through many places. He did not let Scrooge rest or wait anywhere.

"I understand that this place is where I will live in the future," said Scrooge. "I see the house. Let me see what I shall be in the future!"

The Spirit stopped, and its hand was not pointed at the house.

"The house is over there," Scrooge exclaimed. "Why do you point away?"

The Spirit continued to point at the same thing.

Scrooge ran to the window of his office and looked in. It was an office still but not his. The furniture was not the same, and the figure in the chair was not Scrooge. The Spirit still pointed in the other direction.*

He followed the Spirit again, and wondering why it was going this way, he followed it until they reached an iron gate. He stopped to look around before entering. They were in a churchyard.*

argue 언쟁하다, 말다툼하다 **direction** 방향, 방위 **churchyard** (교회의) 뜰, 경내

Here was where the dead man was buried. Here was where he would learn his name. It was not a nice graveyard.* No one cut the grass or planted nice flowers here.

The Spirit stood among the graves, and pointed down to one. He approached it, shaking. The Spirit not changed, but Scrooge feared it more than before.

"Before I look at this stone, please tell me something," said Scrooge. "Are these shadows of things that will be or only things that may be?"

Still the Spirit pointed downward to the grave by which it stood.

"Men are likely to have some futures," said Scrooge. "But if a man changes, he will have a different future, right? Tell me this is true before I look at this stone!"

The Spirit still did not move or speak.

Scrooge crept* toward it, shaking as he went. Following the finger, he read on the stone of the neglected* grave his own name, Ebenezer Scrooge.

"Am I that man who lay on the bed?" he cried on his knees.

The finger pointed from the grave to him, and back again.

"No, Spirit!" cried Scrooge. "Oh, no, no!"

The finger still was there.

"Spirit!" he cried, while tightly grabbing its robe. "Hear me! I am not the man I was. I will not be the man who dies alone. Why do you show me this, if I have no hope?"

For the first time the hand of the Spirit seemed to shake.

"Good Spirit, I know you have a kind heart," said Scrooge. "I know you pity me. Promise me that I can change these things if I change my life!"

---

graveyard 묘지, 묘소 **creep** 기다, 포복하다 **neglected** 등한시된, 방치된

The kind hand shook.

"I will honor* Christmas in my heart and try to keep it all the year. I will live in the Past, the Present, and the Future. The Spirits of all Three shall live inside me. I will listen to the lessons that they teach. Oh, tell me I may erase the writing on this stone!"

In his pain, he grabbed the Spirit's hand. The Spirit tried to free its hand. Finally, because the Spirit was stronger, it pulled its hand away from Scrooge. Holding up his hands in a last prayer to change his future, he saw the Spirit change. It shrunk and turned into a bedpost.*

Chapter 05

The End of It

잠이 깬 스크루지는 아직 자신에게 기회가 있음을 알고 안도한다.
다른 사람이 된 스크루지는 커다란 칠면조를 밥 크래칫의 집으로 보내고
저녁에는 조카인 프레드를 방문하여 깜짝 놀라게 한다.

Yes! It was his bed! Best and happiest of all, he had time to change his life!

"I will live in the Past, the Present, and the Future!" Scrooge repeated as he jumped out of bed. "The Spirits of all

honor 기리다, (명절을) 쇠다 **bedpost** 침대 기둥

Three shall live within me. Oh, Jacob Marley! Heaven and the Christmas Time be praised for this! I say it on my knees, old Jacob, on my knees!"

He was so happy and so glowing* with his good ideas that his broken voice would barely come out. He had been weeping so much when he argued with the Spirit that his face was wet with tears.

"They are not stolen," cried Scrooge, folding* one of his bed curtains in his arms. "No one has stolen my bed curtains. They are here. I am here. The shadows of the things that might happen might be changed. They will be. I know they will!"

His hands were busy touching all of his clothes, turning them, putting them on, tearing* them, and dancing with them.

"I don't know what to do!" cried Scrooge, laughing, crying, and behaving like a fool. "I am as light as a feather.* I am as happy as an angel. I am as merry as a schoolboy.* A merry Christmas to everybody! A happy New Year to all the world! Hello here! Whoop! Hello!"

He ran into the living room and was now standing there, out of breath.

"There's my soup!" cried Scrooge, running around to the fireplace. "There's the door through which the Ghost of Jacob Marley entered! There's the corner where the Spirit of Christmas Present sat! There's the window where I saw the wandering spirits! It's all right. It's all true. It all happened. Ha, ha, ha!"

Really, for a man who had not laughed for years, it was a great laugh, a bright laugh. The beginning of many new laughs!

"I don't know what day of the month it is!" said Scrooge. "I don't know how long

---

glowing 열중한, 열렬한 **fold** 접다, 접어 포개다 **tear** 쥐어뜯다 **feather** 깃털
schoolboy 남학생

I've been with the Spirits. I don't know anything. I'm quite a baby. Never mind. I don't care. I'd rather be a baby. Hello! Whoop! Hello here!"

He realized what time it was by the sound of the church bells ringing. Clash! Clang! Ding! Dong! Ding! Dong! Clang! Clash! Oh, wonderful, wonderful!

Running to the window, he opened it and put out his head. There was no fog, and no mist. It was clear, bright, joyful, fresh, and cold. It was the kind of cold that gave people energy. There was golden sunlight, the heavenly* sky, sweet fresh air, and merry bells. Oh, wonderful! Wonderful!

"What date is it?" cried Scrooge, calling downward to a boy in Sunday clothes.

"Eh?" said the boy, who looked surprised.

"What date is it today, my fine boy?"

said Scrooge.

"Today?" said the boy. "It's Christmas Day."

"It's Christmas Day!" said Scrooge to himself. "I haven't missed it. The Spirits have done it all in one night. They can do anything they like. Of course they can. Of course they can. Hello, my fine boy!"

"Hello!" replied the boy.

"Do you know the butcher's shop in the next street at the corner?" Scrooge asked.

"Yes, I do," replied the boy.

"An intelligent* boy!" said Scrooge. "An amazing boy! Do you know whether they've sold the big turkey that was hanging up there? Not the little turkey, the big one?"

"What, the one as big as me?" asked the boy.

heavenly 거룩한, 신성한 **intelligent** 총명한, 재치 있는

"What a delightful boy!" said Scrooge. "It's a pleasure to talk to you. Yes, my boy!"

"It's hanging there now," replied the boy.

"Is it?" said Scrooge. "Go and buy it."

"I don't believe you!" exclaimed the boy.

"No, no, I am being honest," said Scrooge. "Go and buy it, and tell them to bring it here, so I can tell them where to take it. Come back with the man, and I'll give you money. Come back with him in less than five minutes, and I'll give you even more money!"

The boy ran off quickly.

"I'll send it to Bob Cratchit's!" whispered* Scrooge, rubbing his hands and laughing. "He won't know who sent it. It's twice the size of Tiny Tim!"

The hand in which he wrote the address was shaking, but he barely wrote it anyway and went downstairs to open the street door. He was ready for the turkey to come. As he stood there, waiting for his arrival, the knocker caught his eye.*

"I shall love it as long as I live!" cried Scrooge, touching it with his hand. "I never looked at it before. What an honest face it has! It's a wonderful knocker! Here's the turkey! Hello! Whoop! How are you? A merry Christmas!"

It was a wonderful turkey! When the turkey was alive, he was probably too fat to stand!

"Why, it's impossible to carry that to Camden Town," said Scrooge. "You must have a cab."

He laughed while he said this, and laughed while he paid for the turkey, and laughed while he paid for the cab. He laughed while he paid the boy. Yet

---

whisper 속삭이다 **catch one's eye** 눈길을 끌다

he laughed the most when he sat down breathless in his chair again and laughed till he cried.

Shaving* was not easy, for his hand continued to shake very much. But even if he had cut the end of his nose off, he would have still felt quite satisfied.*

He dressed himself in his best clothes and at last* got out into the streets. The people were by this time coming out of their houses, as he had seen them with the Spirit of Christmas Present. As he walked with his hands behind him, Scrooge looked at everyone with a delighted smile.

He looked so pleasant that three or four kind men said, "Good morning, sir! A merry Christmas to you!" And Scrooge said often afterward* that they were the happiest sounds he ever heard.

He had not gone far, when he saw the fat gentleman coming toward him. He was the one who had walked into his office the day before, and said, "Scrooge and Marley's, I believe?" It made him feel pain to imagine what this man must think about him.

"My dear sir," said Scrooge, walking faster and taking the fat gentleman by both his hands. "How do you do? I hope you succeeded yesterday. It was very kind of you. A merry Christmas to you, sir!"

"Mr. Scrooge?" said the fat man.

"Yes," said Scrooge. "That is my name, and I fear it may not be pleasant to you. I am sorry. And will you have the goodness...." Scrooge started whispering in the man's ear.

"Lord bless me!" cried the gentleman, surprised. "My dear Mr. Scrooge, are you serious?"

---

shaving 면도 **satisfied** 만족한 **at last** 마침내 **afterward** 나중에

"If you please," said Scrooge. "I will not give any less. Will you do me that favor?"

"My dear sir," said the gentleman, shaking hands with him. "I don't know what to say to such...."

"Don't say anything, please," replied Scrooge. "Come and see me. Will you come and see me?"

"I will!" cried the gentleman. And it was clear he wanted to, too.

"Thank you," said Scrooge. "I thank you fifty times. Bless you!"

He went to church, walked around the streets, and watched the people running, and touched children on the head. He questioned beggars, looked down into the kitchens of houses, and up to the windows, and found that everything could make him happy. He had never dreamed that any walk, that anything, could give him so much happiness. In the afternoon, he walked toward his nephew's house.

He passed the door a dozen times before he had the courage* to go up and knock. But he finally did it.

"Is your master at home, my dear?" asked Scrooge to the girl.

"Yes, sir," she said.

"Where is he, my love?" asked Scrooge.

"He's in the dining room, sir, along with his wife," said the girl. "I'll show you upstairs, if you please."

"Thank you," said Scrooge, with his hand already on the dining room lock.* "He knows me. I'll go in here, my dear."

He turned it gently and opened the door. They were looking at the table, trying to prepare everything for their guests.

"Fred!" said Scrooge.

Scrooge's niece jumped in surprise!

---

courage 용기 **lock** 자물쇠, 잠금 장치

Scrooge had forgotten that she was sitting near the door on her stool.

"Why bless my soul!" cried Fred. "Who's that?"

"It's I, your uncle Scrooge," said Scrooge. "I have come to dinner. Will you let me in, Fred?"

He was in the house in five minutes. Nothing could be happier. His niece looked just the same. So did Topper when he came. So did the sister when she came. So did everyone when they came. There was a wonderful party, wonderful games, and wonderful happiness!

But he was early at the office the next morning. If only he could be there first and catch Bob Cratchit coming late! That was the thing he wanted.

And he did it. Yes, he did! The clock struck nine. Bob was not there. It was a quarter past. There was no Bob. He was eighteen minutes and a half behind his time. Scrooge sat with his door wide open so he might see him come into the office. His hat was off before he opened the door, his blanket too. He was on his stool quickly and began to work.

"Hello!" growled Scrooge, in his normal voice. "Why were you late?"

"I am very sorry, sir," said Bob. "I was late."

"You were?" said Scrooge. "Yes. I think you were. Step this way, sir, if you please."

"It's only once a year, sir," begged Bob, appearing from the office. "It shall not be repeated. I had a busy day yesterday."

"Now, my friend, I'll tell you what I am not happy with the way things are," said Scrooge. "And therefore, I am about to raise your salary*! A merry Christmas,

---

salary 봉급, 급료

Bob!" said Scrooge honestly as he patted* Bob on the back.

Bob looked at his master, embarrassed.

"I'll raise your salary, and try to help your struggling family," said Scrooge. "We will talk about your family over a nice dinner today, Bob! Start the fires!"

Scrooge did everything he promised and more. To Tiny Tim, who did not die, he was a second father. He became a good friend, a good master, and a good man. He became one of the best men in the city, or in the world. Some people laughed to see the change in him, but he let them laugh, and he didn't listen to them.

He was wise enough to know that nothing good on this world ever happened that people didn't laugh at. He realized that these people were ignorant and blind. His own heart laughed, and that was quite enough for him.

He never met another spirit again. People always said that he knew how to celebrate Christmas better than anyone. May all of us learn to celebrate Christmas well! And so, as Tiny Tim said, God bless us, everyone!

---

pat 톡톡 가볍게 치다, 토닥거리다

전문번역

말리의 유령

p.12 말리는 죽었다. 그 점에 관해서는 의심의 여지가 없다. 목사, 서기, 장의사가 모두 말리가 죽었다는 서류에 서명했다. 스크루지도 그 서류에 서명했다. 그리고 스크루지는 사실이 아닌 것에는 절대로 서명하는 일이 없었다. 말리 영감은 완전히 죽었다.

p.13 스크루지는 말리가 죽은 것을 알고 있었을까? 물론 알고 있었다. 어떻게 모를 수 있었겠는가? 스크루지와 말리는 여러 해 동안 동업자였다. 스크루지는 말리의 유일한 변호사였고, 그의 유일한 동료이자 그의 유일한 친구였고, 그리고 그의 장례식의 유일한 조문객이었다. 하지만 스크루지조차도 말리가 죽었다는 것이 아주 슬프지는 않았다. 스크루지는 진정한 사업가였으며 자신이 장례식 가격을 싸게 잘 치렀다고 확신했다.

어쨌든 말리가 죽었다는 것에는 마음속에 조금의 의심의 여지도 없는 것이 분명하다. 만약 말리가 죽었다는 것을 정말로 믿지 않는다면, 내가 여러분에게 말해 주려고 하는 이야기는 덜 경이로울 것이다. 누군가가 죽었다는 것을 믿지 않는다면, 그가 여전히 밤에 밖을 어슬렁거리는 것을 보는 것이 놀랍겠는가? 만약 그의 목소리가 바람결에 속삭이는 소리를 듣는다면 여전히 겁이 날까?

p.14 스크루지와 말리의 이름이 둘 다 여전히 그들의 사무실 건물 문에 페인트로 쓰여 있었다. 스크루지는 그 이름을 지운 적이 없었다. 그 회사는 스크루지와 말리 상점으로 알려져 있었다. 신규 고객들은 때로는 스크루지를 그의 본명으로 불렀고, 또 때로는 그를 말리라고 불렀다. 스크루지는 두 가지 이름에 모두 대답했다. 그것은 스크루지에게 중요하지 않았다.

오! 하지만 스크루지는 인색하고 탐욕스럽고 늙은 구두쇠였다! 스크루지의 심장은 강철처럼 단단했다. 스크루지의 내부에는 그의 코끝과 뺨을 얼어붙게 하는 냉정함이 있었다. 그러한 냉정함은 스크루지를 판자처럼 똑바로 걷게 만들었다. 그러한 냉정함은 스크루지의 눈이 충혈되게 하고 그의 얇은 입술을 파래지게 만들었다. 그러한 냉정함은 스크루지의 목소리조차도 쇳소리가 나고 무정하게 만들었다. 스크루지는 항상 자신의 냉기를 몰고 다녔다. 스크루지는 가장 무더운 여름날에조차도 자신의 사무실을 춥게 만들었고, 심지어는 크리스마스에도 따뜻해진 적이 없었다.

p.15 더위도 스크루지를 따뜻하게 만들 수 없었고, 냉랭한 날씨도 그

를 춥게 하지 못했다. 부는 바람도 스크루지보다 더 가혹하지는 않았다. 내리는 눈이나 비도 스크루지만큼 결단력이 있지는 않았다. 강우나 강설만이 유일하게 스크루지보다 한 가지를 더 잘했다. 때때로 내리고 있는 눈이나 비는 아주 멋있어 보인다. 스크루지는 전혀 멋있어 보이지 않았다.

스크루지에게 인사를 하기 위해 거리에서 그의 발걸음을 멈추게 하는 사람은 여태껏 아무도 없었다. 어떤 거지도 스크루지에게 돈을 구걸하지 않았고, 어떤 아이들도 그에게 시각을 묻지 않았으며, 어떤 남녀도 그에게 길을 묻지 않았다. 맹인견들조차도 스크루지를 아는 것 같았다. 스크루지가 오고 있는 것을 보면, 맹인견들은 자기 주인을 그에게서 떨어지도록 잡아당기려고 했다. 맹인견들은 스크루지의 악의 있는 눈을 두려워했다!

p.16 하지만 스크루지는 상관하지 않았다! 스크루지는 그것이 좋았다! 스크루지는 많은 사람들 사이를 돌아다니며 그들 모두가 자신을 두려워하는 것을 지켜보는 것이 아주 좋았다. 스크루지는 혼자 있는 것이 아주 좋았다.

어느 크리스마스 전날, 스크루지 영감은 자신의 돈을 세느라 분주했다. 춥고 흐리고 위험한 날씨였다. 안개가 너무 짙어서 보는 것이 힘들었다. 자신들이 그곳에 있는 것을 다른 사람들이 알 수 있게 하려고 바깥에 있는 사람들이 발을 구르고 있는 소리를 스크루지는 들을 수 있었다. 고작 오후 3시밖에 안 됐지만, 날은 벌써 어두웠다. 양초들의 희미한 불빛이 사무실 창문에서 빛났다.

안개가 모든 갈라진 틈과 열쇠구멍을 통해 쏟아져 들어왔다. 안개는 아주 짙어서 다른 집들은 유령처럼 보였다. 도시 위에 아주 자욱하게 드리워진 구름을 보고 있는 것은 사람들에게 자연이 무언가 요상한 것을 계획하고 있다고 느끼게 했다. 스크루지의 사무실 문은 열려 있어서 그는 자신의 서기를 볼 수 있었는데, 서기는 작고 음울한 방에서 편지들을 베껴 쓰고 있었다. **p.17** 스크루지는 아주 작은 난롯불을 피우고 있었으나, 서기의 난롯불은 훨씬 더 작아서 단 한 조각의 석탄만 타고 있을 뿐이었다.

스크루지가 자기 사무실에 석탄을 보관하고 있기 때문에 서기는 석탄을 더 얻을 수 없었다. 만약 석탄을 더 원했다가는 스크루지가 자신을 해고할까 봐 서기는 두려웠다. 서기는 자신의 하얀 담요를 몸에 두르고 촛불로 손을 따뜻하게 하려고 애썼다. 서기는 그래도 여전히 추위를 느꼈다.

"즐거운 크리스마스 되세요, 삼촌!" 명랑한 목소리가 들렸다. "주님께서 삼촌을 보살펴 주시기를 빌어요!"

그것은 스크루지의 조카의 목소리였는데, 그는 갑작스럽게 스크루지를 놀랬다.

"흥!" 스크루지가 말했다. "허튼소리!"

p.18 안개 속에서 어찌나 빨리 걸었던지 스크루지의 조카는 덥다고 느꼈다. 조카의 얼굴은 불그스름하고 잘생겼다. 조카의 눈은 반짝였고, 입김이 하얗게 나왔다.

"크리스마스가 허튼소리라고요, 삼촌?" 스크루지의 조카가 말했다. "그런 뜻으로 하신 말씀은 아니라고 제가 믿어도 되죠?"

"그런 의미야." 스크루지가 말했다. "즐거운 크리스마스라고? 네 녀석이 왜 즐거운데? 네 녀석이 즐거워지는 이유가 무엇이 있는데? 가난뱅이 주제에."

"그럼 삼촌이 기분이 안 좋으신 이유는 뭐예요?" 조카가 말했다. "삼촌이 화가 나는 이유로는 무엇이 있는데요? 삼촌은 부자이시면서."

"흥! 허튼소리." 스크루지가 다시 말했다.

"화내지 마세요, 삼촌!" 조카가 말했다.

"바보들의 세상에 살 때 내가 달리 어떤 사람이 될 수 있겠느냐?" 스크루지가 투덜거렸다. "즐거운 크리스마스라고? 크리스마스에 누가 신경을 쓴다고! 크리스마스란 돈이 없을 때 청구서들을 지불해야 하는 때야! p.19 너는 한 살을 더 먹지만 조금이라도 더 잘 살게 되지는 않잖아! 일 년 열두 달이 어떻게 사라지는지에 대해서는 너도 무슨 생각이 들 텐데! 할 수 있다면, 나는 즐거운 크리스마스라고 하는 사람들을 모두 삶아 버릴 거야!"

"삼촌!" 조카가 애원했다.

"조카야, 너는 네 방식대로 크리스마스를 보내라." 스크루지가 말했다. "그리고 내가 내 방식대로 그날을 보내게 놔둬."

"크리스마스에 삼촌께서 이런 말씀을 하시는 것을 들을 수는 없어요." 조카가 말했다.

"그럼 나 좀 혼자 있게 내버려 둬! 내 마음을 바꿔 놓으면 네가 뭐라도 얻을까 봐? 내가 너에게 선물을 줄 것 같으냐?" 스크루지가 말했다.

"제가 무언가를 얻지 못한다고 해서 하나도 덕을 못 본다는 뜻은 아니에요." 조카가 말했다. "다른 사람들이 크리스마스에 대해 어떤 생각을 생각하는지는 상관없지만, 저에게는 그날이 중요해요. p.20 물론 저는 크리스마스를 거룩한 날로써 신경 쓰는 거예요. 하지만 제 가족과 친구들과 정을 나누는 날이기도 해요. 비록 크리스마스가 저에게 금은보화를 준 것은 아니지만, 그래도 저에게 좋은 것들을 주었어요."

서기가 갑자기 박수를 치기 시작했다. 그런 다음 자기 상관이 화낼 것임을 깨닫고 그만두었다. 서기는 멋쩍게 작은 난롯불을 쑤시기 시작했다.

"서기 너 이 녀석, 한 번만 더 시끄럽게 굴면 해고해 버리고 말 테다!" 스크루지가 말했다. "꽤 힘 있는 연설가이시로군요, 조카 나리." 스크루지가 자기 조카 쪽으로 몸을 돌리고 덧붙였다. "정계에 입문해 보시지 그래요?"

"화내지 마세요, 삼촌." 조카가 말했다. "오세요! 내일 저희와 함께 저녁 식사 하세요."

"네 가족과 저녁 식사를 하느니 차라리 나 혼자 먹겠다." 스크루지가 말했다.

"하지만 왜요?" 스크루지의 조카가 소리쳤다. p.21 "왜 그러시는데요?"

"결혼은 왜 했냐?" 스크루지가 물었다.

"사랑에 빠졌으니까요." 조카가 대답했다.

"사랑에 빠졌기 때문이라고!" 마치 세상에서 그 말이 즐거운 크리스마스라는 말보다 더 우스꽝스러운 유일한 말인 것처럼 스크루지가 으르렁거렸다. "오후 잘 보내라!"

"단지 저희가 사랑에 빠져 있기 때문에 저희를 보고 싶지 않으신 거예요?" 조카가 말했다. "그것은 합당한 이유가 아니잖아요."

"가 봐." 스크루지가 말했다.

"저는 삼촌께 바라는 것이 하나도 없어요." 조카가 말했다. "저는 삼촌께 아무것도 부탁하지 않습니다. 왜 우리는 친하게 지낼 수 없죠?"

"그만 가라니까!" 스크루지가 말했다.

"삼촌이 그렇게 황소고집이신 것을 알게 되어 진심으로 유감이에요." 조카가 말했다. "삼촌을 화나게 할 생각은 없었어요. p.22 삼촌을 이해할 수는 없지만, 저는 여전히 삼촌이 즐거운 크리스마스를 보내시면 좋겠어요. 그러면 즐거운 크리스마스 보내세요, 삼촌!"

"어서 가!" 스크루지가 말했다.

"그리고 새해 복 많이 받으세요!" 조카가 말했다.

"어서 가라고!" 스크루지가 말했다.

스크루지의 조카는 성난 말 한마디 하지 않고 사무실을 떠났다. 조카는 서기에게 즐거운 크리스마스를 보내라고 하려고 문간에서 걸음을 멈추었는데, 서기는 비록 몸은 추웠지만 그래도 따뜻하게 답해 주었다.

"바보가 한 명 더 있군." 서기의 목소리를 들은 스크루지가 투덜거렸다. "급여도 적고, 아내와 가족이 있는 서기가 즐거운 크리스마스에 대해 말하고 있다니."

조카를 내보냈을 때 이 미치광이 바보는 두 사람을 안으로 들였다. 그들은 즐거워 보이는 뚱뚱한 신사들이었다. 그들은 스크루지의 사무실에서서 모자를 벗었다. **p.23** 그들은 책과 서류를 손에 들고 있었고 스크루지에게 머리를 숙였다.

"여기가 스크루지와 말리 상점입니까?" 자신의 목록을 바라보며 신사들 중 한 명이 말했다. "제가 스크루지 씨나 말리 씨를 만나 뵐 수 있을까요?"

"말리 씨는 죽은 지 7년이 되었소이다." 스크루지가 대답했다. "말리 씨는 7년 전 바로 오늘 밤에 죽었소."

"말리 씨의 동업자이신 선생님께서 말리 씨가 하고 싶어 하셨던 것을 하시리라고 저희는 믿어 의심치 않습니다." 그 신사가 자신의 신분증명서를 보여 주며 말했다.

사실 스크루지와 말리는 아주 비슷했다. 스크루지는 신분증명서를 보고 나서 그 신사를 다시 쳐다보았다.

"지금이 크리스마스 때이니까요, 스크루지 씨." 두 신사 중 한 명이 말했다. "우리가 무언가를 가난한 사람들에게 주는 것이 평소보다 지금 더 중요합니다. **p.24** 그들은 지금 크게 고통을 받고 있습니다. 수많은 사람들이 음식, 물, 집 같은 기본적인 것들을 가지고 있지 못합니다. 수많은 사람들이 위로를 필요로 하지요."

"감옥은 하나도 없소?" 스크루지가 물었다.

"감옥은 많습니다." 신사가 자신의 펜을 내려놓으며 말했다.

"그러면 구빈원들은?" 스크루지가 덧붙였다. "여전히 운영 중이오?"

"그렇습니다." 신사가 말했다. "그렇지 않다고 말씀드릴 수 있으면 좋겠습니다만."

"구빈원에 있거나 감옥에 갇혀 있는 가난한 사람들이 많소?" 스크루지가 물었다.

"네, 아주 많습니다." 신사가 대답했다.

"오!" 스크루지가 말했다. "당신이 처음 말했던 것에서 바뀐 것이 있을까 봐 걱정했었소. 그 소리를 들으니 아주 기쁘군."

"가난한 사람들에게는 크리스마스 정신도 또한 크리스마스 기분도 없습니다." 신사가 말했다. p.25 "저희를 중 몇 명이 가난한 사람들에게 고기, 음료수, 그리고 따뜻한 담요와 옷을 사 줄 돈을 모금하고자 애쓰고 있습니다. 지금이야말로 어느 때보다도 가난한 사람들이 일상생활에 필요한 물품들을 정말로 원하는 때이기 때문에 저희는 이때를 고른답니다. 선생님은 무엇을 주고 싶으십니까?"

"아무것도 없소!" 스크루지가 대답했다.

"저희가 선생님의 성함을 꼭 적어야 하는 것은 아닙니다." 신사가 말했다. "만약 선생님께서 저희에게 돈을 주신 것을 다른 사람들이 아는 것을 원하지 않으신다면, 익명으로 주실 수 있습니다."

"나는 혼자 있고 싶소." 스크루지가 말했다. "당신이 내가 원하는 것이 무엇인지 물으니까 말하는데, 신사 양반, 그것이 나의 대답이오. 나에게는 즐거운 크리스마스는 없고, 다른 사람들을 크리스마스에 즐겁게 느끼게 해 주고 싶지도 않소. 나는 감옥과 구빈원을 후원하는 것을 돕는다오. p.26 가난한 사람들은 그곳에 가면 되오!"

"소수의 사람들만 그곳에 갈 수 있습니다." 신사가 말했다. "또한 많은 사람들이 그곳에 가느니 차라리 죽어 버리겠다고 한답니다."

"차라리 죽어 버리겠다면, 그럼 죽으면 되겠네." 스크루지가 말했다. "그런 식으로 우리는 인구를 줄일 수 있소이다. 이 나라에는 이미 지나치게 많은 사람들이 있거든."

"우리는 모두 가난한 사람들을 도와야 합니다." 신사가 말했다.

"그것은 내 알 바 아니오." 스크루지가 말했다. "나는 내 몸을 돌보지. 나는 항상 내 자신을 돌보느라 바쁘오. 잘 가시오, 신사 양반!"

계속 부탁하는 것이 소용없을 것임을 분명히 알았기 때문에 신사들은 스크루지의 사무실을 떠났다. 자기 자신에게 높은 평가를 내리며 스크루지는 다시 일을 계속했다.

그사이 안개와 어둠이 너무 짙어져서 사람들은 등불을 들고 거리를 이리저리 뛰어다녔다. 스크루지의 사무실 창문을 통해 언제나 그를 몰래 지켜보던 오래된 교회 탑은 이제 눈에 보이지 않았다. p.27 저 높이 구름 속에서 교회 종이 울렸다. 마치 추위에 떨고 있는 이빨이라도 달린 것처럼 종은 덜덜 떨리는 소리를 냈다. 추위는 점점 더 심해졌다.

큰 거리의 마을 광장 한 구석에서 몇몇 일꾼들이 가스관을 수리하고 있었다. 그들은 큰 불을 피웠고, 그 불 주위에는 한 무리의 가난한 남자들과 소년들이 모여 있었다. 그들은 그곳에서 즐거워하며 그들의 손을 녹였다. 거리에 있던 물은 갑자기 얼음으로 변했다. 상점의 밝은 불빛들은 사람들의 창백한 얼굴을 불그스름하게 만들었다.

정육점과 식품점들은 그들의 상품들을 팔면서 즐거워하기 시작했다. p.28 크고 웅장한 집에 사는 시장은 자신의 50명의 주방장과 집사들에게 집으로, 가족들에게 가라고 말했다. 거리에서 주로 소란을 일으키던 몸집이 작은 재단사조차도 크리스마스 푸딩을 만들며 집에 있었다. 그러는 동안 재단사의 아내와 아이는 고기를 사러 갔다.

여전히 안개는 점점 더 자욱해지고 날씨는 추워졌다. 살을 에고 파고드는 듯한 추위였다. 만약 늑대와 곰들이 여전히 런던에 살고 있다면 그 동물들조차도 이러한 밤에는 추위를 느꼈을 것이었다. 몹시 허기지고 지독하게 추위를 느끼는 어떤 젊은이가 스크루지의 사무실 문을 두드렸다. 그 젊은이는 스크루지에게 크리스마스 캐럴을 불러 주고 싶어 했다.

"주님께서 아저씨를 축복해 주시기를, 유쾌한 신사 아저씨!" 문을 열었을 때 젊은이가 스크루지에게 노래를 불러 주었다. "그대에게 슬픔을 가져다줄 것은 아무것도 없기를!" 스크루지가 어찌나 빨리 자를 움켜잡았던지 젊은이는 혼비백산하여 도망쳤다.

마침내 사무실 문을 닫고 집으로 갈 시간이 되었다. p.29 스크루지는 화를 내며 의자에서 내려왔고 서기에게 집에 가라고 말했다. 서기는 촛불을 끄고 자신의 모자를 썼다.

"자네, 내일은 가족들과 함께 집에 있고 싶겠지?" 스크루지가 말했다.

"네, 그럴 수 있다면요." 서기가 말했다.

"나는 자네가 그러지 않았으면 하네." 스크루지가 말했다. "그리고 그것은 공정하지가 않아. 자네가 일했는데 내가 봉급을 주지 않는다면 자네는 화가 나겠지?"

서기는 희미하게 미소를 지었다.

"하지만 자네가 일하지 않는다고 하더라도 크리스마스 하루치 일당을 내가 주게 되어 있어." 스크루지가 말했다.

"일 년에 딱 한 번뿐입니다, 사장님." 서기가 말했다.

"그것은 매년 12월 25일에 내 돈을 가져가려는 형편없는 변명이야!" 스크루지가 자신의 큰 외투의 단추를 채우며 말했다. p.30 "하지만 자네는 하루 종일 쉴 것이 틀림없을 것 같군. 그 다음날 아침에는 더 일찍 나오게."

서기는 그러겠다고 약속했으며, 스크루지는 툴툴대며 밖으로 나갔다. 사무실은 신속하게 닫혔다. 하얀 담요를 허리에 두른 서기는 거리를 통과해 집으로 달려갔다. 서기는 가능한 한 빠르게 집으로, 자기 가족에게 돌아갔다.

스크루지는 자신이 평소에 가는 음울한 선술집에서 음울한 저녁 식사를 했다. 모든 신문을 읽고, 자신의 예금 통장을 쳐다보는 데 남은 저녁나절을 보낸 후, 스크루지는 잠을 자러 집으로 갔다. 스크루지는 한때 자신의 죽은 동업자의 소유였던 방들 중 하나에서 살았다. 그 방들은 침울한 방들의 한 세트였다. 이러한 장소에 집을 가지고 있는 것은 이상했는데, 그 집이 주변의 다른 건물들과 아주 달라 보였기 때문이었다. 그 집은 이제 오래되고 쓸쓸하고 음침했는데, 스크루지 외에는 아무도 그 집에 살지 않기 때문이었다. 다른 방들은 모두 사무실들이었다.

p.31 마당은 너무 어두워서 그곳의 돌 하나까지도 알고 있는 스크루지조차도 길을 찾으려고 손을 사용했다. 안개와 서리가 마치 검은색 현관문 그 자체에 의해 만들어져 있는 듯 검은색 현관 주변에 매달려 있었다. 아무튼 현관의 쇠고리에 관해서는 그것이 아주 크다는 것 외에는 특별한 것이 아무것도 없었다.

사실, 스크루지는 이 집에서 생활하는 매일 아침저녁으로 이 쇠고리를 봐 왔다. 또한 스크루지에게는 상상력이 거의 없었고 공상에 잠긴 적도 한 번도 없었다. 게다가 그날 오후에 죽은 지 7년 된 동업자에 대해 마지막으로 언급한 이후로는 말리에 대해서 생각한 적도 없었다. 이후에 무슨 일이 일어났던 거였는지 그 누가 설명할 수 있겠는가? 문의 자물쇠를 열 때, 스크루지는 쇠고리에 있는 말리의 얼굴을 보았던 것이다.

p.32 그것은 분명 말리의 얼굴이었다. 그 얼굴은 마당에 있는 다른 물체들처럼 어두운 그림자 아래에 있지는 않았으나, 지하실에 있는 썩은 바닷가재처럼 주변에 희미한 빛을 뿜고 있었다. 그것은 화가 나 있거나 위험하지는 않았지만, 말리가 예전에 스크루지를 바라보았던 것처럼 그를 바라보았다.

유령의 얼굴은 모양이 분명하지 않은 이마에 모양이 분명하지 않은 안경을 걸치고 있었다. 머리카락은 바람에 날린 것처럼 이상하게 흐트러져 있었다. 또한 비록 눈을 크게 부릅뜨고 있었지만, 움직이지 않았다. 그런 점은, 그리고 그 얼굴의 보기 흉한 색깔은 그 얼굴을 끔찍하게 보이게 만들었다. 유령의 얼굴은 끔찍해지는 것을 원하지 않는 듯했지만 실제로는 끔찍했다. 스크루지는 이 유령을 빤히 쳐다보았고, 그것은 다시 쇠고리가 되었다.

스크루지가 놀라지 않았다거나 그의 심장이 빨리 뛰고 있지 않았다고 말하는 것은 사실이 아닐 것이다. 하지만 스크루지는 떨어뜨렸던 열쇠에 손을 올렸고 그것을 자물쇠에 넣고 돌려 문을 열고 안으로 들어갔다.

p.33 스크루지는 문을 닫기 전에 잠시 생각을 해 보려고 정말로 멈춰 섰다. 그렇게 하기 전에 스크루지는 마치 문 반대편에서 말리를 보게 될 거라고 절반쯤 기대하는 듯 먼저 문 뒤를 주의 깊게 살펴보았다. 하지만 문 뒤에는 쇠고리를 지탱하고 있는 나사와 너트 외에는 아무것도 없었다.

"흥, 제기랄!" 스크루지는 말하고 쾅 소리가 나게 문을 닫았다.

문이 닫히는 소리는 천둥소리 같았다. 위에 있는 모든 방, 그리고 아래쪽 포도주 상인의 창고에 있는 모든 병들이 약간 흔들리는 것 같았다. 스크루지는 소리에 깜짝 놀라는 사람이 아니었다. 스크루지는 천천히 문을 잠갔고, 홀을 가로지르고, 계단 위로 올라갔다. 스크루지는 가면서 촛불을 들고 있었다.

p.34 층계는 아주 넓어서 여전히 여유 공간이 있었다. 이것이 아마도 스크루지가 어둠 속에서 자신을 지나쳐 계단 위쪽으로 운행하는 영구차가 달려 있는 기차를 보았다고 생각한 이유이리라. 여섯 개의 가로등조차도 계단을 잘 밝히지 못했을 테니까 스크루지의 작은 촛불은 간신히 길을 밝힐 뿐이었다.

하지만 스크루지는 어둠에는 신경 쓰지 않고 계속해서 계단을 올라갔다. 스크루지는 돈이 덜 드니까 어두운 것을 좋아했다. 하지만 자기 방의 육중한 문을 닫기 전에, 스크루지는 모든 것이 괜찮은지 살펴보려고 방을 가로질러 걸어갔다. 말리의 얼굴에 대한 기억은 스크루지가 조심하도록 분위기를 조장했다.

거실, 침실, 창고는 모두 원래 있어야 할 그대로였다. 탁자 아래에는 아무도 없었고, 소파 아래에도 아무도 없었다. 작은 불이 벽난로 안에 피워져 있었고, 숟가락과 냄비가 준비되어 있었으며, 작은 죽 그릇이 책상 위에 있었다. p.35 침대 아래에도 아무도 없었고, 벽장 안에도 아무도 없었으며,

벽에 으스스하게 걸려 있는 스크루지의 목욕 가운 안에도 아무도 없었다. 모든 것은 정상이었다.

무척 만족한 상태로 스크루지는 문을 닫고 안에서 문을 잠갔다. 스크루지는 심지어 두 번째 자물쇠까지 잠갔는데, 이는 그가 대체로 하지 않는 일이었다. 그렇게 하여 더 안전해졌다는 기분을 느끼며 스크루지는 옷을 갈아입고 난롯불 앞에서 죽을 먹었다.

그것은 이렇게 지독하게 추운 밤에는 아주 작은 불이었다. 따뜻하다고 느끼기 위해서 스크루지는 불에 아주 바싹 붙어 앉아야 했다. 벽난로는 오래 전에 어떤 네덜란드 상인에 의해 만들어진 오래된 것이었다. 벽난로는 성경에서 발췌한 몇몇 이야기에 토대를 둔 그림을 그린 타일로 장식되어 있었다. p.36 그 타일들 위에는 카인과 아벨, 파라오의 딸들, 시바의 여왕들, 그리고 깃털 침대 같은 구름 위에서 공중을 떠도는 천사들이 있었다. 그 위에는 또한 스크루지가 생각해 낼 수 있는 수많은 아름다운 작은 그림들이 있었다.

그러나 죽은 지 7년 된 말리의 그 얼굴이 스크루지가 생각할 수 있는 유일한 것이었으며 그의 눈에 보이는 것 같은 유일한 것이었다. 만약 각각의 매끄러운 타일이 텅 비어 있었더라면, 스크루지는 모든 타일에 그려져 있는 말리 영감의 머리를 상상했을 것이었다.

"말도 안 돼!" 스크루지는 말했고, 방을 가로질러 걸어갔다.

몇 차례 그런 다음, 스크루지는 다시 앉았다. 의자에 달린 의자받이에 머리를 털썩 뒤로 기댔을 때, 스크루지의 시선은 우연히 방 안에 매달려 있는 오래된 종에 머무르게 되었다. 오랫동안 사용되지 않았던 이 종이 갑자기 울리기 시작했다. 대단히 놀랍게도, 이 종은 흔들리기 시작했다. 종은 처음에는 아주 부드럽게 흔들려서 간신히 소리가 났다. p.37 하지만 곧 종이 크게 울렸고, 집 안에 있는 모든 종들이 요란하게 울렸다.

이는 30초 혹은 1분 동안 지속됐을 뿐이었지만, 1시간은 계속된 것 같았다. 종들은 울리기 시작했을 때처럼 일제히 멈췄다. 다음에 스크루지는 저 아래 깊은 땅속에서 나오는 철거덕거리는 소리를 들었다. 마치 어떤 사람이 포도주 창고에 있는 병들 위로 무거운 쇠사슬을 끌고 있는 듯한 소리가 났다. 그때 스크루지는 귀신이 나오는 집들에 있는 유령들에 관해 들었던 것이 기억났다. 그 유령들은 쇠사슬을 끌고 다니는 것으로 묘사되어 있었다.

지하실 문은 쿵 하는 소리와 함께 활짝 열렸으며, 그런 다음 스크루지는 아래에 있는 층들에서 훨씬 더 큰 소리를 들었다. 그런 다음 그 소리는 층계로 올라오고 있었다. 그런 다음 그 소리는 스크루지의 방문을 향해 곧장 다가오고 있었다.

p.38 "여전히 말이 안 되잖아!" 스크루지가 말했다. "나는 안 믿을 거야."

무엇인가가 문을 통해 날아 들어왔을 때, 스크루지의 얼굴은 완전히 하얗게 질렸다. 유령이 방으로 들어오자 불꽃이 피어올랐다가 사그라졌다.

"나는 그를 알아!" 불꽃이 말하는 듯했다. "그것은 말리의 유령이야!"

그것은 말리의 유령이었다. 그 유령의 얼굴은 말리의 얼굴과 정확히 똑같았다. 유령에게는 말리의 머리카락이 달려 있었고 말리의 바지, 말리의 재킷, 말리의 긴 장화를 착용하고 있었다. 유령이 끌고 온 쇠사슬은 그의 허리에 둘러져 있었다. 그 쇠사슬은 길었고 꼬리처럼 그의 등에서부터 매달려 있었다. 그 쇠사슬은 금고, 열쇠, 자물쇠, 서류, 무거운 강철 손가방으로 만들어져 있었다. 유령의 몸은 다 들여다보였다. 유령을 보았을 때, 스크루지는 유령의 재킷 앞뒤의 단추들을 둘 다 볼 수 있었다.

스크루지는 종종 말리의 속이 텅 비어 있다는 말을 들었지만, 지금까지는 이 말을 믿지 않았다. p.39 그렇다. 심지어는 지금도 그 말을 믿지 않았다. 비록 유령을 응시했고, 유령이 자기 앞에 서 있는 것을 보았지만, 그리고 심지어는 죽어서 생기 없는 유령의 눈빛의 냉기를 느꼈음에도 불구하고, 스크루지는 여전히 유령을 믿지 않았다. 스크루지는 여러 차례 자기 눈을 감았으며 유령이 사라지기를 바라고자 애썼다.

"도대체 어떻게 된 일인가?" 스크루지가 평소처럼 냉정하고 심술궂게 말했다. "나에게 무슨 볼 일이 있는 건가?"

"많이 있지!" 말리의 목소리가 말했는데, 그 점에 대해서는 틀림이 없었다.

"너는 누구야?" 스크루지가 물었다.

"내가 누구였냐고 물어야지." 말리의 목소리가 대답했다.

"그럼 자네는 누구였나?" 목소리를 높이며 스크루지가 말했다. "유령치고 자네는 이상하군."

하지만 스크루지가 어떻게 알겠는가? 이 유령은 스크루지가 처음 만난 유령이었다.

p.40 "현세에서 나는 자네의 동업자 제이콥 말리였네." 유령이 말했다.

"자네, 앉을 수 있나?" 스크루지가 의심의 눈초리로 유령을 바라보며 물었다.

"그럴 수 있네." 유령이 말했다.

"그럼 앉게." 스크루지가 말했다.

스크루지는 유령이 실제로 의자에 앉을 수 있는지 없는지 몰랐기 때문에 그 질문을 했다. 만약 그것이 불가능하다면, 유령은 당황할 것이고 긴 변명을 해야 할 것이라고 스크루지는 느꼈다. 하지만 유령은 마치 그것에 익숙해진 듯이 벽난로 맞은편에 앉았다.

"자네는 내 존재를 믿지 않는군." 유령이 말했다.

"안 믿네." 스크루지가 말했다.

"하지만 자네는 나를 보고, 내 목소리를 듣고, 나를 느낄 수 있지 않은가?" 유령이 말했다. "왜 나를 못 믿지?"

p.41 "잘 모르겠네." 스크루지가 말했다.

"왜 자네의 감각을 의심하지?" 유령이 물었다.

"감각은 거짓말을 할 수 있으니까." 스크루지가 말했다. "약간의 복통은 존재하지 않은 것을 보이게 할 수 있지. 자네는 약간의 상한 소고기, 조금 상한 겨자, 치즈 부스러기, 혹은 썩은 감자 조각일 수도 있어. 자네는 단지 열 때문에 사람에게 보이는 무언가일 수도 있네!"

대체로 스크루지는 실제로 복통에 걸리는 일이 없었다. 사실은 스크루지가 똑똑하게 굴려고 애썼다는 것이다. 스크루지는 말리의 유령에 관해 생각하지 말아야 했으므로 변명거리를 생각해 내고자 애썼다. 말리의 유령은 스크루지가 뼛속까지 깊이 끔찍한 냉기를 느끼게 했다.

만약 앉아서 잠시라도 움직이지 않는 눈을 쳐다보고 있다가는 미쳐 버릴 것이라고 스크루지는 생각했다. p.42 말리의 유령이 그 자신의 냉기로 만들어 낸 방법에 대해서도 무언가 아주 끔찍한 것이 있었다. 말리의 유령은 또한 자신이 만들어 낸 바람을 가지고 있는 듯했다. 비록 유령은 가만히 앉아 있었지만, 말리의 유령의 옷은 여전히 그의 발밑에서 부는 바람에 날리는 것처럼 가만히 움직였다.

"이 이쑤시개가 보이지?" 스크루지가 말했다. 스크루지는 말리의 유령이 자신을 바라보지 않고 그 대신 다른 무언가를 바라보게 하려고 애썼다.

"보이네." 말리의 유령이 대답했다.

"보고 있지 않잖아." 스크루지가 말했다.

"하지만 어쨌든 나는 그것이 보이네." 말리의 유령이 말했다.

"좋아! 내가 이것을 삼키면, 나는 죽을지도 몰라." 스크루지가 말했다. "그러면 나는 자네처럼 밖에 있는 유령들 대신 나를 괴롭히는 내 생각을 갖게 될 테지. 그러니까 허튼소리야! 허튼소리라고!"

이 말에 말리의 유령이 무시무시하게 소리치고 스크루지가 앉아 있던 의자를 꽉 잡을 만큼 크고 끔찍한 소음을 내며 쇠사슬을 흔들었다. p.43 스크루지는 자신이 정신을 잃는 것을 막아야 했다. 그런 다음 말리의 유령은 실내에서 두르고 있기에는 너무 덥다는 듯이 붕대를 끄르기 시작했다. 갑자기 유령의 아래턱이 가슴 위까지 툭 내려앉았다.

스크루지는 무릎을 꿇고 유령의 얼굴 앞에서 자신의 손을 마주잡았다.

"자비를 베풀어 주게!" 스크루지가 말했다. "무시무시한 유령이여, 왜 나를 괴롭히나?"

"세속적인 생각을 하는 인간아!" 말리의 유령이 대답했다. "자네는 나를 믿는가, 안 믿는가?"

"믿네." 스크루지가 말했다. "믿어야지. 하지만 유령들이 왜 이승을 떠돌고, 왜 나에게 오는 것인가?"

"모든 인간들은 다른 인간들과 함께 돌아다니고 멀리 여행을 해야 하네. 인간이 사는 동안 돌아다니고, 여행하고, 다른 사람들에게서 배우지 않으면, 죽은 후에 그 일을 해야 할 거야. p.44 슬퍼하며 이승을 떠돌고 지금은 가질 수 없는 모든 것을 봐야 하네. 가졌을 수도 있었지만 이제는 함께 나눌 수 없는 모든 행복을 보아야 하는 거야."

또 다시 말리의 유령은 소리를 지르고 자신의 그림자 같은 손으로 큰 소리를 내며 쇠사슬을 흔들었다.

"자네는 허리에 쇠사슬을 두르고 있군." 스크루지가 벌벌 떨며 말했다. "왜 그런 것인지 말해 주게."

"나는 내가 이승에서 만들어 놓은 쇠사슬을 두르고 있네." 말리의 유령이 대답했다. "고리 하나씩, 그러다가 1야드씩 이 쇠사슬을 만들었지. 이 쇠사슬을 만드는 것은 나의 선택이었고 그것을 두르는 것도 내 선택이었어. 유령의 방식이 자네에게는 낯선가?"

스크루지는 점점 더 몸을 떨었다.

"아니면 자네가 가지고 다니는 튼튼한 쇠사슬의 무게와 길이를 알겠는가?" 말리의 유령이 말했다. "나의 쇠사슬은 내가 7년 전에 죽은 이후로 변한 것이 없다네. 자네의 쇠사슬도 꼭 이것과 같지만, 길이는 더 길지."

스크루지는 자기 주변과 마룻바닥을 둘러보았다. 스크루지는 자신의 몸 주위나 방 안의 어딘가에서 쇠사슬을 볼 거라고 예상했지만, 아무것도 보이지 않았다.

p.45 "제이콥." 스크루지가 간청했다. "제이콥 말리, 나에게 좀 더 말해 주게. 나에게 위로가 되는 말을 해 주게, 제이콥!"

"나는 해 줄 말이 하나도 없네." 유령이 대답했다. "그 말은 나보다 더 행복한 삶을 살았던 다른 유령들에게서 나온다네. 나는 자네에게 말해 주고 싶은 것을 모두 자네에게 말해 줄 수도 없네. 자네에게 몇 가지만 말해 줄 수 있을 거야. 나는 쉴 수 없네. 나는 머무를 수가 없네. 나는 어디에서도 살 수 없네. 살아 있을 때, 나는 우리 집이나 우리 사무실보다 더 멀리 가 본 적이 없었지. 그래서 이제 나는 쉬지 않고 멀리 있는 곳을 많이 여행해야 한다네."

무슨 생각을 하기 시작할 때마다 스크루지는 손을 자기 바지 주머니 안에 집어넣었다. 여전히 무릎을 꿇고 앉아 있는 동안, 스크루지는 말리의 유령이 한 말에 관해 아주 곰곰이 생각해 보았다.

p.46 "자네는 분명히 아주 천천히 돌아다니고 있었나 보군." 스크루지가 사업가 같은 말투로 말했다. 하지만 스크루지의 목소리는 평소보다 더 소심했다.

"천천히라고!" 말리의 유령이 따라 말했다.

"자네가 죽은 지 7년이 되었군." 스크루지가 말했다. "그리고 여전히 여행하는 것을 끝내지 못하고 있고!"

"내내 휴식도 없고, 평화도 없었어. 나는 언제나 후회로 무척 고통 받고 있지." 말리의 유령이 말했다.

"빠르게 다니기는 하나?" 스크루지가 물었다.

"바람의 날개를 타고 다녀." 유령이 대답했다.

"그렇다면 7년 동안 분명히 많은 장소를 다녀왔겠군." 스크루지가 말했다.

이 말을 듣자마자 말리의 유령은 소리를 지르고 아주 큰 소리를 내며 쇠사슬을 흔들었다. 말리의 유령이 너무 시끄러워서 경찰이 와서 이 고요한 밤에 너무 많은 소음을 낸 것에 대하여 유령을 체포할지도 모를 일이라고 스크루지는 생각했다.

p.47 "오, 그래, 여태 돌아다녔지!" 말리의 유령이 소리쳤다. "나는 내

내 쇠사슬을 차고 돌아다녔어. 살아 있는 사람들이 죽은 후에 평화를 찾기 위해 얼마나 기다려야 하는지 알면 좋을 텐데! 내가 놓친 아주 많은 기회들이 있었지. 나는 내가 살았던 짧은 생애 중 아주 많은 시간을 허비했어! 하지만 그것은 내가 한 선택이야! 그리고 지금 나는 고통을 겪어야 해."

"하지만 자네는 언제나 훌륭한 사업가였어, 제이콥." 이제 자신이 말리와 똑같은지 궁금해지기 시작한 스크루지가 말했다.

"사업!" 말리의 유령이 다시 손을 흔들며 소리쳤다. "내 사업은 인간을 위한 것이었지. 사람들 돕기, 자선, 자비, 친절과 연민이 나의 일이었어. 우리 회사를 위해 번 돈은 나의 진정한 사업의 아주 작은 부분에 불과했어!"

p.48 말리의 유령은 마치 자신을 묶은 쇠사슬이 모든 고통과 후회의 원인이라는 듯 그것을 자기 앞에 들어올렸다. 그런 다음 쇠사슬을 다시 바닥에 힘껏 던졌다.

"한 해의 이맘때쯤이면 나는 가장 고통을 받지." 말리의 유령이 말했다. "내가 왜 많은 사람들 사이를 다니면서도 그들의 얼굴을 쳐다보지 않았던가? 내가 왜 도움이 필요한 사람들을 도울 생각을 전혀 하지 않았던가? 내가 왜 다른 사람들의 문제를 무시했을까?"

말리의 유령이 말하고 있는 것들에 스크루지는 몹시 당황했다. 스크루지는 자신의 온몸이 떨리고 전율하는 것을 느꼈다. 스크루지는 유령의 얼굴을 바라볼 수 없었다.

"내 말을 듣게!" 말리의 유령이 소리쳤다. "내게 주어진 시간이 거의 다 지나갔네."

"그러겠네." 스크루지가 말했다. "하지만 나를 심하게 대하지는 말게. 나를 다치게 하지는 말게, 제이콥! 제발!"

"오늘 밤에 자네가 나를 보게 된 이유를 나는 자네에게 말해 줄 수 없네." 유령이 말했다. "사실 나는 여러 번 자네 옆에 앉아서 자네를 지켜보았지만, 그때 자네는 나를 볼 수 없었다네."

p.49 이러한 생각은 스크루지를 행복하게 만들지 않았다. 스크루지는 와들와들 떨고 이마의 땀을 훔쳤다.

"대체로 나는 눈에 보이지 않게 된 것을 즐기지 못한다네." 말리의 유령이 말을 이어갔다. "그것은 내가 받는 형벌의 일부야. 나는 오늘 밤 자네에게 경고를 해 주러 여기 있는 것이네. 자네는 나와 같은 운명을 피할 기회와 희망을 여전히 가지고 있네. 에브니저, 나는 이 기회와 희망에 대해 자네에게 말해 주려고 여기 온 것이라네."

"자네는 언제나 나에게 좋은 친구였네." 스크루지가 말했다. "고마워!"

"자네에게 세 명의 유령이 붙을 것이네." 말리의 유령이 말을 계속했다.

스크루지의 고개가 떨어졌고, 스크루지는 또 다시 말리의 유령을 쳐다볼 수가 없었다.

"그것이 자네가 설명한 기회와 희망인가, 제이콥?" 스크루지가 떨리는 목소리로 물었다.

p.50 "그렇다네." 말리의 유령이 대답했다.

"나, 나는 안 그러는 것이 나을 것 같네." 스크루지가 말했다.

"그들이 방문을 하지 않는다면 자네한테는 희망이 없어." 말리의 유령이 경고했다. "자네는 나처럼 될 것이네. 내일 1시에 시계가 친 후 첫 번째 유령을 기다리게."

"그냥 그들을 모두 동시에 만나고 끝낼 수는 없겠나, 제이콥?" 스크루지가 물었다.

"두 번째 유령은 그 다음날 밤 같은 시각에 기다리게." 말리의 유령이 말했다. "세 번째 유령은 그 다음날 밤 12시를 알리는 마지막 종이 울리는 것을 멈출 때 찾아올 것이네. 자네는 나를 더 이상 보지 못할 거야! 하지만 내가 자네에게 말해 준 것을 자네는 꼭 기억해야 하네! 자네가 스스로를 구원하고 싶다면 그것이 도움이 될 것이네."

이 말을 할 때, 말리의 유령은 탁자에서 붕대를 가져가 그것을 전처럼 자기 머리에 감았다. 말리의 유령이 턱을 원래 있어야 할 자리로 돌려놓았을 때 이가 일제히 딱딱거리는 소리를 냈다. p.51 쇠사슬을 자신의 팔에 감은 채 서 있는 말리의 유령을 보려고 스크루지는 천천히 다시 위를 올려다보았다.

말리의 유령은 스크루지로부터 뒷걸음질을 쳤다. 말리의 유령이 한 발 한 발 발을 디딜 때마다 창문이 조금씩 저절로 올라갔다. 유령이 창문에 다다랐을 때 창문은 활짝 열렸다. 말리의 유령은 더 가까이 오라고 스크루지를 불렀으며, 그는 그렇게 했다. 그들이 서로 두 발자국 거리에 떨어져 있게 되었을 때 말리의 유령은 손을 들고 더 이상 가까이 오지 말라고 경고했다. 스크루지는 멈추어 섰다.

유령과 이렇게 가까이 있었기 때문에, 스크루지는 많은 것들의 소리를 들었다. 스크루지는 자신의 허비된 삶을 후회하는 많은 유령들의 울부짖

음을 들었다. 스크루지는 그들의 고통과 그들의 공포를 들었다. 스크루지는 그들의 고통의 절규를 들었다. 이 유령은, 잠시 귀를 기울인 후, 역시 비명을 지르기 시작했고 고요하고 어두운 밤하늘을 둥둥 떠다니며 날아갔다. p.52 스크루지는 매우 호기심을 느끼며 창문으로 달려갔다. 스크루지는 밖을 내다보았다.

대기는 빠르게 이곳저곳을 떠돌아다니고 있고 지나가면서 울고 있는 유령들로 가득했다. 그들 모두는 말리의 유령처럼 쇠사슬을 차고 있었다. 유령들 중 일부는 서로 묶여 있었다. 쇠사슬 중 일부는 더 길거나 더 짧았으나, 그들 중 아무도 자유롭지 않았다. 스크루지는 유령들의 얼굴 중 일부를 알아보았다.

스크루지는 흰 외투를 입고 발목에 거대한 철제 금고를 매달고 있는 늙은 유령과 아주 친했었다. 그 유령은 아래쪽에 있는 문들 중 어떤 문 밖에 앉아 있는 살아 있는 여인과 그 여인의 갓난아기를 도울 수가 없어서 큰 소리로 울었다. 유령들의 가장 큰 괴로움은 그들이 인간들을 오로지 지켜보기만 할 수 있다는 점인 것이 분명했다. 그들은 살아 있는 사람들에게 혹은 그들과 함께 무엇이든 할 수 있는 힘을 영원히 잃어버린 것이었다.

p.53 이런 산물들이 안개 속으로 사라진 것인지, 혹은 안개가 그들을 뒤덮은 것인지, 스크루지는 분간할 수 없었다. 하지만 유령들과 그들의 영적 목소리들도 함께 희미해졌다. 밤은 다시 고요해졌다.

스크루지는 창문을 닫고 유령이 들어왔던 문을 바라보았다. 그 문은 자기 손으로 잠갔을 때처럼 이중으로 잠겨 있었고, 자물쇠들은 변한 것이 없어 보였다. 스크루지는 "말도 안 돼!"라고 말하려고 애썼지만, 맨 처음 소리에서 말이 막혔다. 시간이 참 많이 늦었고, 자신이 본 모든 유령들 때문에 참 많이 지친 데다가 자신의 미래가 참 많이 두려웠기 때문에 스크루지에게는 휴식이 아주 많이 필요했다. 스크루지는 옷도 갈아입지 않고 곧장 침대에 들어 즉시 곯아떨어졌다.

세 유령들 중 첫 번째 유령

p.54 스크루지가 깨어났을 때는 너무 어두워서 벽에 있는 창문이 간신히 보일 뿐이었다. 근처의 교회에서 종소리가 울리는 것이 들었을 때 스크루지는 어둠 속을 보려고 애쓰고 있는 중이었다. 그래서 스크루지는 시간

을 알아보려고 귀를 기울였다.

대단히 놀랍게도, 육중한 종소리는 여섯 번째에서 일곱 번째로 갔고, 그리고 일곱 번째에서 여덟 번째로 갔으며, 규칙적으로 열두 번째까지 울리더니 멈췄다. **p.55** 12시라니! 스크루지가 잠자리에 들었을 때는 2시가 지나서였다. 시계가 틀린 것이었다. 얼음이 종을 고장 낸 것이 분명했다. 12시라니! 스크루지는 자기 시계를 찾으려고 책상 위를 바라보았다. 그 시계의 빠르고 작은 맥박도 열두 번을 치고 멈췄다.

"이런, 내가 하루를 꼬박 자고 또 다음날 밤까지 잘 수 있었다는 것은 가능하지 않아." 스크루지가 말했다. "태양에 무슨 일이 일어났다는 것도 불가능하고 지금이 정오라는 것도 불가능하잖아."

이러한 생각은 너무나도 충격적이어서 스크루지는 침대에서 뛰쳐나와 창문으로 더듬더듬 다가갔다. 스크루지는 자신의 잠옷 소매로 서리를 문질러 없애고 나서야 비로소 무언가를 볼 수 있었으며 여전히 아주 조금만 보였다. 스크루지가 볼 수 있는 전부는 여전히 아주 안개가 자욱하고 춥다는 것이었다. **p.56** 낮이지만 날이 여전히 어둡기만 한 것이었다면 분명히 시끄러운 소리가 났을 터였지만, 그때는 이리저리 뛰어다니는 사람들에게서 나오는 시끄러운 소리는 없었다. 이 때문에 스크루지는 다소 기분이 나아졌다. 만약 태양이 비추는 것을 멈춘다면 무슨 일이 일어날지 스크루지는 상상도 할 수 없었다.

스크루지는 다시 침대로 가서 생각에 생각을 거듭해 보았지만, 어떠한 이유도 생각해 낼 수 없었다. 더 많이 생각할수록, 스크루지는 더욱 혼란스러워졌다. 생각하지 않으려고 하면 할수록 스크루지는 더 많이 생각하게 되었다.

말리의 유령은 스크루지를 많이 성가시게 했다. 스크루지는 유령의 차가운 태도 혹은 움직이지 않는 눈에 대한 생각을 그만둘 수 없었다. 스크루지는 그것이 단지 꿈이었을 뿐이라고 매번 스스로에게 말했지만, 그의 마음은 계속해서 혹시 그것이 꿈이 아니었는지 궁금해 하고 있었다.

"그것이 꿈이었을까 아니었을까?" 스크루지는 스스로에게 질문을 했다.

스크루지는 이러한 상태로 45분이 지날 때까지 누워 있었다. **p.57** 그런 다음 갑자기 말리의 유령이 1시에 다른 유령이 올 것이라고 경고한 것이 기억났다. 스크루지는 그 시간이 지나갈 때까지 깨어 있기로 마음먹었는데, 어쨌든 자신이 잠들 수 있으리라고는 생각하지 않았기 때문에 그 일은 쉬웠다.

그 15분이 어찌나 길던지 스크루지는 자신이 잠이 들어 시계 소리를 못 들은 것이 틀림없다고 몇 차례나 생각했다. 마침내 시계가 울리기 시작했다.

"그 시각이 되었는데도 다른 유령은 안 나타나잖아!" 스크루지가 의기양양하게 말했다. 스크루지가 말하자마자 예정된 시각을 알리는 종이 깊고 음울하게 울렸다. 즉시 빛이 방 안을 번쩍 비추었고, 스크루지의 침대 커튼이 열렸다.

스크루지의 침대 커튼은 어떤 손에 의해 옆으로 젖혀졌다. 스크루지의 발치에 있는 커튼도, 그의 등 쪽에 있는 커튼도 아니었지만, 스크루지의 얼굴은 그 커튼 쪽으로 움직여졌다. p.58 스크루지는 일어나 앉았고 이상한 유령 같은 형상과 마주쳤다.

그것은 이상한 형상이었다. 그것은 아이처럼 보이기도 하고 노인처럼 보이기도 했다. 목 주위에 늘어져 등까지 떨어진 그 형상의 머리카락은 많은 나이 때문에 하얗게 쇠었으나, 얼굴에는 주름살 하나 없었다. 그 형상의 뺨조차 붉은 장밋빛이었다. 팔과 손은 길고 근육질이었다. 그것은 그 형상을, 특히 튼튼해 보이게 만들었다.

그 형상의 다리와 발은 연약해 보였고 옷 아래에 감추어져 있지 않았다. 그 형상은 순백색의 셔츠를 입고 있었고 허리에는 반짝이는 아름다운 허리띠를 차고 있었다. 그 형상은 손에 싱싱한 초록색 서양호랑가시나무 가지를 들고 있었다. 그 형상의 옷 끝자락은 여름 꽃들로 장식되어 있었다.

하지만 그 형상과 관련해 가장 이상한 것은 머리끝에서부터 밝고 투명한 빛이 난다는 것이었다. p.59 그 빛은 방 전체를 비추었다. 그 형상은 또한 그 빛을 감추기 위해 사용할 수 있는 모자를 가지고 다녔다.

하지만 그 형상을 응시했을 때, 스크루지는 이것조차도 그 형상과 관련해 가장 이상한 점은 아니라는 것을 깨달았다. 한순간 허리띠가 반짝반짝 빛났다가 어두워졌다. 갑자기 그 형상은 팔이 하나인 형상이었다가 이제 다리가 하나였다가, 이제는 다리가 스무 개였고, 이제는 머리 없이 다리가 한 쌍이었다가, 이제는 몸통 없이 머리가 하나였다. 이렇게 각기 다른 신체 부위들이 어둠 속으로 사라졌다가 다시 원래의 모습처럼 보였다.

"이봐요, 당신이 나를 방문하기로 되어 있는 유령입니까?" 스크루지가 물었다.

"그렇네!" 유령이 말했다.

목소리는 부드럽고 상냥했다. 그 목소리는 스크루지의 가까운 곳에서 나는 대신 멀리서 들렸다.

p.60 "당신은 누구이며 무슨 일을 합니까?" 스크루지가 물었다.

"나는 과거의 크리스마스 유령이라네." 유령이 말했다.

"먼 과거인가요?" 스크루지가 물었는데, 유령이 어떤 신비한 산물처럼 보였기 때문이었다.

"아니야. 너의 과거이다." 유령이 말했다.

이유는 몰랐지만, 스크루지는 갑자기 그 유령이 모자를 쓰고 있는 것이 보고 싶었다. 스크루지는 유령에게 그렇게 해 달라고 부탁했다.

"뭐라고!" 유령이 고함을 쳤다. "너는 왜 내가 주는 빛을 보고 싶어 하지 않는 것이냐? 네가 이 모자를 만드는 것을 도왔던 사람들 중 하나라는 것으로는 충분하지 않으냐? 너는 내가 때때로 그 모자를 가지고 다니며 써야 하는 이유들 중 하나이다."

"당신이 무슨 말을 하고 있는 것인지 나는 모르겠습니다." 스크루지가 말했다. "나는 모자를 만든 적도, 혹은 당신을 전에 만난 적도 없습니다. 당신은 왜 이곳에 있는 것입니까?"

"너를 위해서이다!" 유령이 말했다.

p.61 "아, 고맙군요." 스크루지는 대답했지만, 실은 차라리 자는 것이 더 낫겠다고 생각하고 있었다. 유령은 스크루지가 생각하고 있는 것을 들은 것이 분명했다.

"너는 내 말에 귀를 기울여야 해!" 유령이 그 즉시 말했다.

유령은 말을 할 때 자신의 힘센 손을 내밀어 스크루지의 팔을 부드럽게 잡았다.

"일어서라!" 유령이 말했다. "그리고 나와 함께 걷자!"

스크루지는 밤이 늦었다고 불평할 수도 있었다. 스크루지는 밖이 꽁꽁 얼듯이 춥고 자신은 얇은 잠옷만을 입고 있을 뿐이며 신발도 안 신었다고 불평할 수도 있었다. 하지만 그것은 소용없을 것이었다. 비록 유령의 손은 여인의 손처럼 부드러웠지만, 스크루지는 유령에게 저항할 수 없었다. 스크루지는 일어섰지만, 그들이 창문으로 걸어갔을 때 유령은 멈추어 섰다.

p.62 "나는 못 날아요." 스크루지가 속삭였다. "나는 추락할 거예요."

"걱정 마라." 유령이 말했다. "나를 믿어라. 너는 날 수 있을 것이다!"

그 말이 나왔을 때, 그들은 벽을 통과해서 양쪽에 밭이 펼쳐진 탁 트인 시골길 위에 서 있었다. 도시는 사라졌다. 어둠과 안개 역시 도시와 함께 사라졌는데, 땅에 눈이 쌓인 맑고 추운 겨울날이기 때문이었다.

"맙소사!" 스크루지가 자기 주변을 둘러보면서 손뼉을 치고 말했다. "나는 이곳에서 자랐어요! 이곳에서 나는 소년이었다고요!"

유령은 스크루지를 조용히 응시했다. 스크루지는 여전히 유령의 부드러운 손길을 느낄 수 있었다. 스크루지는 공중을 떠다니는 수많은 다른 냄새를 맡았다. 각각의 향기마다 오랫동안, 오랫동안 잊었던 수천 가지 생각, 희망, 기쁨, 그리고 걱정과 연결되어 있었다!

"네 입술이 떨리고 있구나." 유령이 말했다. p.63 "그리고 네 뺨에 있는 그것은 무엇이냐?"

"뾰루지일 뿐이에요." 스크루지가 투덜거렸다.

"이 길이 기억나느냐?" 유령이 물었다.

"기억납니다!" 스크루지가 열렬하게 소리쳤다. "눈가리개를 쓰고도 그곳을 걸어 다닐 수 있었지요."

"그런데 왜 그렇게 오랜 세월 동안 그 길을 잊고 있었느냐?" 유령이 물었다. "계속 가 보자."

그들은 길을 따라 걸었고, 스크루지는 모든 문, 말뚝, 그리고 나무를 알아보았다. 멀리서 시장이 서는 작은 마을이 다리와 교회와 꾸불꾸불한 강과 함께 나타났다. 털이 수북하게 난 몇 마리의 조랑말이 농부가 모는 짐수레에 탄 다른 소년들을 소리쳐 부르는 소년들을 등에 태우고 그들 쪽으로 다가가고 있었다. 이 모든 소년들은 아주 행복했고 넓은 들판이 즐거운 음악으로 가득 찰 때까지 서로에게 소리쳤다.

p.64 "이것들은 존재해 온 것들의 환영일 뿐이다." 유령이 말했다. "그들은 우리가 이곳에 있는 것을 모른다."

사람들이 지나갈 때, 스크루지는 모든 사람을 알고 있어서 그들의 이름을 불렀다. 그들 모두를 보게 되어 스크루지의 마음에는 기쁨이 넘쳤다. 그들이 지나갈 때 스크루지의 무정한 눈이 반짝반짝 빛났고 그의 심장은 빠르게 뛰었다. 그들이 서로에게 즐거운 크리스마스를 기원하는 것을 들었을 때 스크루지는 왜 기쁜 마음이 가득했을까? 즐거운 크리스마스란 스크루지에게 무엇이었을까? 즐거운 크리스마스는 꺼지라지! 그것이 스크루지에게 무슨 좋은 일을 해 주었다고?

"학교에 아직 인적이 끊긴 것은 아니군." 유령이 말했다. "친구들에게 따돌림 당하는 외로운 아이가 아직 그곳에 남아 있어."

스크루지는 그것을 안다고 말했다. 그리고 흐느꼈다.

그들은 큰길을 떠나 기억이 생생한 어느 길에 들어섰다. 곧 그들은 칙칙한 붉은 벽돌집에 다가갔다. p.65 지붕에는 종이 하나 달려 있었다. 그것은 커다란 집이었으나, 음울해 보였다. 커다란 사무실들은 전혀 사용되지 않았고, 벽들은 축축하고 이끼가 끼어 있었으며, 창문들은 깨어져 있었고, 현관들은 썩어 있었다. 닭들이 마구간에서 꼬꼬 소리를 냈고, 창고 안에는 자라난 긴 풀들이 있었다.

내부라고 더 나아 보이지는 않았다. 만약 누군가가 들어와서 방 안을 들여다보았다면, 그 방들에 고작 가구 몇 점만 있고 춥고 아주 넓기만 하다는 것을 발견했을 것이었다. 차가운 공기 속에는 흙냄새가 났다.

유령과 스크루지는 홀을 가로질러 집 뒤에 있는 문으로 갔다. 문은 그들 앞에서 열렸고 간소한 책상과 의자들이 있는 길쭉하고 음침한 방을 보여 주었다. p.66 이 중 한 곳에서는 외로워 보이는 소년이 불꽃이 약한 난롯불 근처에서 책을 읽고 있었다. 예전에 그랬던 것과 같은 불쌍하고 기억에서 사람들에게서 잊힌 자기 자신을 보고 스크루지는 앉아서 울었다.

벽 뒤에서 나는 쥐들이 찍찍거리는 소리도, 밖의 수도꼭지에서 똑똑 물 떨어지는 소리도, 집 밖의 다 떨어진 나무에서 나는 바람 소리도, 흔들리는 문에서 나는 소리도, 혹은 난롯불 안에서 타닥거리는 소리도 스크루지가 울 때 그를 위로해 주지 못했다.

유령은 스크루지의 팔을 툭 치고 그의 어린 자아를 가리켰는데, 그는 여전히 책을 읽고 있었다. 갑자기 놀랄 만큼 진짜 같은 외국 옷을 입은 한 남자가 창 밖에 서 있었다. 그는 허리띠에 도끼를 꽂고 있었고 당나귀를 끌고 있었다.

"이런, 저 사람은 알리바바예요!" 스크루지가 소리쳤다. "다정하고 정직한 알리바바 영감님이요! 그래요, 나는 알아요! 어느 크리스마스 날, 외로운 아이가 이곳에 혼자 남겨졌을 때, 알리바바 영감님이 처음으로 오셨어요! p.67 가엾은 녀석! 그리고 밸런타인과 그의 난폭한 형제인 오슨도요! 그들이 저기로 가네요! 그리고 저 사람의 이름이 뭐더라? 자다가 죽은 사람 말이에요! 저 사람이 보이지 않아요? 그가 있었다니 기뻐요! 어떻게 그가 공주와 결혼할 수 있었을까요?"

스크루지가 울고 웃으며 알리바바와 다른 동화들에 대해 이야기하는 것을 들었다면 다른 사업가들은 충격에 빠졌으리라.

"초록색 몸통에 노란 꼬리가 달리고 정수리에서 자라는 상추처럼 생긴 것이 달린 앵무새가 있어요. 저기 그 사람이 있어요! 가엾은 로빈슨 크루소! 로빈슨 크루소가 섬 주변을 항해한 후 다시 집에 왔을 때, 앵무새가 '가엾은 로빈슨 크루소, 어디 갔었어요, 로빈슨 크루소?'라고 말했어요. p.68 그 남자는 자신이 꿈을 꾸고 있다고 생각했지만, 그렇지 않았죠. 오, 저기 프라이데이가 걸음아 나 살려라 하고 작은 강으로 달려가네요!"

스크루지는 자신의 어린 시절에 연민을 느꼈다.

"가엾은 녀석!" 스크루지가 다시 외쳤다.

순식간에 스크루지의 표정 전체가 변했고 스크루지는 더 이상 신나 보이지 않았다. 대신에 스크루지는 슬퍼 보였다.

"이제 너무 늦었어요." 스크루지가 조용히 투덜거리고 자신의 손을 주머니에 넣었다.

"뭐가 문제지?" 유령이 물었다.

"아무것도요." 스크루지가 말했다. "아무것도요. 어젯밤에 제 사무실 문 앞에서 크리스마스 캐럴을 부르던 젊은이가 있었어요. 그 젊은이에게 무언가 주었더라면 좋았을 텐데. 그것이 다예요."

"다른 크리스마스를 살펴보자." 유령이 생각에 잠긴 듯 미소를 지으며 손을 흔들면서 말했다.

유령이 이 말을 하자마자 스크루지의 어린 자아는 점점 커졌고, 방은 약간 더 어두워지고 더 더러워졌다. p.69 벽에 붙어 있는 목재는 더 작아졌고, 창문은 금이 갔으며, 천장 조각들은 떨어졌다. 다른 아이들이 모두 즐거운 휴가를 보내러 집으로 가 버렸을 때 소년은 그곳에 다시 혼자 있었다.

이제 소년은 책을 읽고 있지는 않았지만 낙담한 채 이리저리 걸어 다니고 있었다. 스크루지는 유령을 쳐다보았고, 고개를 슬프게 흔들며 근심하며 문 쪽을 바라보았다. 문이 열리고 소년보다 훨씬 더 어린 소녀가 안으로 달려 들어왔다. 소녀는 소년의 목에 팔을 두르고 입을 맞추었다.

"사랑하는 오빠." 작은 손으로 손뼉을 치고 허리를 구부려 깔깔 웃으면서 소녀가 소년에게 말했다. "오빠를 집에 데려가려고 왔어, 사랑하는 오빠! 오빠를 집으로 데려가려고 말이야, 집으로!"

p.70 "집이라고, 팬?" 소년이 말했다.

"그래!" 소녀가 행복감으로 충만하여 말했다. "집으로, 영원히. 집으로 완전히 영원히 말이야. 아버지는 전보다 아주 훨씬 더 친절하셔. 집은 천국 같아! 어느 맑은 밤에 내가 잠을 자러 가는데 아버지가 나에게 아주 다정하게 말을 거셔서 오빠가 집에 와도 되는지 다시 아버지한테 묻는 것이 나는 두렵지 않았어. 아버지는 '그래, 그래야지.'라고 말씀하셨어. 아버지는 오빠를 데려오게 하려고 나를 마차에 태워 주셨어. 그리고 오빠는 어른이 될 거야! 오빠는 이곳에 다시는 돌아오지 않을 테지만, 먼저 우리는 크리스마스 내내 함께 있고 세상에서 가장 즐거운 시간을 보내게 될 거야."

"너는 어른이 다 되었구나, 팬!" 소년이 소리쳤다.

소녀는 손뼉을 치고 웃었다. 소녀는 소년의 머리를 만지려고 애썼지만, 그녀는 너무 작았다. 소녀는 다시 웃고 소년을 껴안으려고 일어섰다. 그런 다음 소년을 문 쪽으로 열심히 끌어당기기 시작했다. p.71 소년은 행복하게 소녀를 따라갔다.

"스크루지의 상자를 그곳에 내려놔!" 무시무시한 목소리가 홀 안에서 외쳤다. 홀에 교장이 모습을 드러냈는데, 그는 스크루지를 무섭게 쳐다보았다. 교장은 스크루지와 악수를 했는데, 이는 스크루지를 정말로 긴장하게 만들었다.

그런 다음 교장은 소년과 소년의 누이동생을 아주 화려하고 중요해 보이는 방으로 데려갔는데, 그곳에는 벽에 있는 지도와 창가에 있는 지구본이 가짜 같고 차가워 보였다. 이곳에서 교장은 이상할 정도로 묽은 포도주 한 병과 이상할 정도로 진한 케이크 조각을 꺼내 왔다. 교장은 어린아이들에게 먹으라고 말했다.

스크루지의 트렁크가 옮겨지기 위해 마침내 끈으로 묶였다. 아이들은 교장에게 행복하게 작별 인사를 하고 방을 떠났다. p.72 그들은 마차에 탔고 정원을 지나 마차는 행복하게 길 아래로 달렸다. 마차가 거리를 요리조리 달릴 때 바퀴와 말들의 발굽은 물을 튀겼다.

"저 아이는 늘 아주 허약했지." 유령이 말했다. "하지만 넓은 마음을 가지고 있었었어!"

"네, 그랬어요!" 스크루지가 외쳤다. "유령님 말이 맞아요. 반대하지 않겠어요, 유령님!"

"저 아이는 어른이 되어 죽었고, 내 생각에는 자식이 있었던 것 같은데." 유령이 말했다.

"한 명 있죠." 스크루지가 말했다.

"맞아." 유령이 말했다. "네 조카지!"

"그래요." 스크루지가 짧게 대답했다. 스크루지는 마음이 불편한 것 같았다.

비록 방금 학교를 뒤로 하고 떠났지만, 그들은 이제 도시의 분주한 거리에 있었다. 그곳에서는 흐릿하게 보이는 행인들이 지나다녔고 흐릿하게 보이는 크고 작은 마차들이 앞 다투어 달렸다. 거리는 정말로 복잡하고 더러웠다. **p.73** 상점 안의 장식물들 때문에 이곳 역시 다시 크리스마스 무렵인 것이 분명했다. 저녁이었고 거리에는 불이 밝혀져 있었다.

유령은 어느 큰 상점 문 앞에 멈추어 섰고 스크루지에게 그곳을 아는지 물었다.

"그곳을 아느냐고요?" 스크루지가 말했다. "이곳에서 사업가가 되는 법을 배운 걸요!"

그들은 안으로 들어갔다. 그들은 큰 키에 비해서는 너무 작아 보이는 의자에 앉아 있는 가발을 쓴 한 노인을 보았다.

"이런, 페찌위그 영감님이잖아!" 스크루지가 외쳤다. "세상에! 페찌위그 영감님이 다시 살아나다니!"

페찌위그 영감은 펜을 내려놓고 시계를 올려다보았는데, 그 시계는 7시를 가리키고 있었다. 페찌위그 영감은 자신의 손을 비비고, 외투를 매만졌다. **p.74** 영감은 온몸으로 웃었다.

"이봐, 자네들! 에브니저! 딕!" 페찌위그 영감이 편안하고 넉살 좋고 즐거운 목소리로 소리쳐 불렀다. 이제 성인이 된 청년인 스크루지의 그 옛날 자아가 재빨리 방에 들어왔고, 다른 견습생이 그 뒤를 따라왔다.

"저 녀석은 딕 윌킨스네요!" 스크루지가 유령에게 말했다. "맙소사, 그래요. 저기 저 녀석이 있네요. 저 녀석은 저를 정말 좋아했어요. 가엾은 딕! 저런!"

"이봐, 자네들!" 페찌위그 영감이 말했다. "오늘 밤은 더 이상 일이 없어. 크리스마스이브잖아, 딕. 크리스마스야, 에브니저! 창문을 닫자."

그들이 얼마나 빨리 갔는지 믿지 못할 것이다! 하나, 둘, 셋 하는 소리에 그들은 덧문들이 있는 거리로 달려갔고, 넷, 다섯, 여섯에 덧문들을 원래 있던 자리인 위쪽으로 올렸고, 일곱, 여덟, 아홉에 덧문들을 닫았다. 그들은 경주마처럼 숨을 몰아쉬며 돌아왔다.

"좋았어!" 페찌위그 영감이 높은 책상에서 뛰어내리며 소리쳤다. **p.75** "방을 치우게, 자네들, 그리고 여기에 많은 공간을 마련하세! 어서 와, 딕! 가세, 에브니저!"

방을 치워라! 페찌위그 영감이 지켜보는 가운데 그들이 치우지 않을 것도, 혹은 그들이 치우지 못할 것도 없었다. 그것은 순식간에 이루어졌다. 옮길 수 있는 모든 것은 더 이상 아무도 그것을 필요로 하지 않을 것처럼 꾸려져서 치워졌다. 바닥을 쓸고 물을 끼얹고 등불을 켰고 장작이 난롯불 위에 쌓였다. 상점은 아주 편안하고 따뜻하고 뽀송뽀송하고 환한 무도회장이었다.

바이올린을 켜는 사람이 악보집을 가지고 들어왔다. 그는 책상 맨 위에 올라가 연주를 시작했다. 페찌위그 부인이 환한 미소를 지으며 들어왔다. **p.76** 페찌위그 집안의 세 딸들이 미소를 지으며 귀여운 모습으로 들어왔다. 그 딸들에게 애를 태우는 여섯 명의 젊은이들이 들어왔다.

상점에 고용된 모든 젊은이와 여인들이 들어왔다. 하녀가 빵장수인 사촌과 함께 들어왔다. 요리사가 자기 오빠의 친한 친구인 우유 배달부와 함께 들어왔다. 자기 주인에게 충분히 급료를 받지 못하는 소년이 길 건너에서 들어왔다. 그 소년은 옆집 소녀의 뒤에 몸을 숨기려고 했다.

어떤 사람은 부끄러워하며, 어떤 사람은 대담하게, 어떤 사람은 우아하게, 어떤 사람은 어색하게, 어떤 사람은 밀면서, 어떤 사람은 잡아당기면서, 그들은 차례차례 안으로 들어왔다. 그들은 모두 그들이 들어올 수 있는 모든 방법으로 안으로 들어왔다. 그들이 모두 들어오니 스무 쌍이었다. 그들은 모두 큰 무리를 이루고 줄을 서서 함께 춤을 추려고 했다. 때때로 그들은 실수를 했고, 이상해 보이기도 했다. 또 어떤 때에는 완벽하게 춤을 추었다.

p.77 마침내 그들이 완벽하게 춤을 추었을 때, 페찌위그 영감은 춤을 중단시키려고 손뼉을 쳤다.

"잘했어!" 페찌위그 영감이 소리쳤다. 바이올린 켜는 사람은 자신의 달아오른 얼굴을 물 단지에 넣었다. 아직 춤추는 사람들은 없었지만, 바이올린 켜는 사람은 쉬지도 않고 즉시 다시 연주하기 시작했다.

더 많은 춤을 추었고 케이크가 있었고, 음료가 있었고, 커다란 소고기 덩어리가 있었고, 커다란 생선 토막이 있었고, 파이가 있었고, 많은 맥주가 있었다. 하지만 그날 저녁의 최고의 순간은 저녁 식사 후에 이어졌다. 이것은 바이올린 켜는 사람이 아주 인기 있는 곡을 연주하기 시작한 때였다.

그런 다음 페찌위그 영감이 페찌위그 부인과 함께 춤을 추기 시작했다. 그들은 최고의 댄싱 커플이기도 했다. p.78 그들은 모든 젊은이들보다 더 춤을 잘 추었다. 그들은 걸을 수 있는 것보다 춤출 수 있는 것을 더 잘할 수 있는 부류의 사람들이었다.

설령 춤추는 사람들의 수가 두 배가 되었다고 하더라고 페찌위그 영감은 여전히 그들보다 더 나았을 것이고 페찌위그 부인도 그랬을 것이다. 페찌위그 부인으로 말하자면, 페찌위그 영감만큼이나 훌륭한 춤꾼이었다. 아름다운 불빛이 페찌위그 영감의 다리에서 나오는 듯했다. 그 다리는 춤을 추는 모든 동작에 달처럼 빛을 비추었다. 사람들은 페찌위그 부부가 다음에 무엇을 하려고 했는지 짐작할 수 없었을 것이다. 그리고 페찌위그 영감과 페찌위그 부인이 춤을 끝냈을 때, 페찌위그 영감은 높이 뛰었다가 완벽하게 착지했다.

시계가 11시를 쳤을 때, 파티는 끝났다. 페찌위그 부부는 문 양쪽에 서서 사람들이 나갈 때 모든 사람과 개별적으로 악수를 했다. 그들은 또한 사람들에게 즐거운 크리스마스를 보내라고 기원해 주었다. p.79 두 명의 견습생을 제외하고 모든 사람이 떠났을 때, 그들 부부는 견습생들에게도 똑같이 행동했다. 그렇게 쾌활한 목소리들이 잦아들었다. 청년들은 가게 뒤의 카운터 밑에 있는 자신들의 잠자리에 들었다.

이 시간 동안 내내 스크루지는 몹시 신이 나 있었다. 스크루지의 마음과 정신은 자신의 젊었을 적 자아와 함께했다. 스크루지는 모든 일에 대해 생각해 보았고 모든 일을 추억했으며, 모든 일을 즐겼는데, 이상하게 짜증이 났다. 자신의 이전의 자아와 딕의 밝은 얼굴이 변하고 나서야 비로소 스크루지는 유령이 기억났고 유령의 머리 위의 빛이 아주 밝게 빛나는 동안 유령이 자신을 쳐다보고 있었다는 것을 깨달았다.

"이 어리석은 사람들을 행복하게 해 주는 것은 아주 쉬운 것 같군." 유령이 말했다.

p.80 "쉽다고요!" 스크루지가 말했다.

유령은 두 명의 견습생을 가리켰는데, 그들은 페찌위그 영감을 칭찬하고 있었다.

"이런, 안 그렇다고?" 유령이 말했다. "영감은 이 파티에 약간의 돈을 썼을 뿐이야. 왜 영감이 그렇게 많은 칭찬을 들을 만한 거지?"

"그런 게 아니에요." 스크루지가 화가 나서 자신의 늙은 자아가 아니라 어린 자아처럼 말했다. "그런 것이 아니라고요, 유령님. 페찌위그 영감님은 우리를 행복하게 하거나 불행하게 하는 힘을, 우리의 일을 가볍게 하거나 부담스럽게 하는 힘을, 그리고 우리가 기쁨을 느끼게 하거나 괴로움을 느끼게 하는 힘을 가지고 있어요. 영감님의 힘은 말과 표정에 담겨 있어요. 그 힘은 아주 사소하고 작은 것들에 담겨 있어서 더하거나 셈을 할 수가 없지요. 영감님이 우리에게 주는 행복은 큰 재산과 같은 것이에요."

스크루지는 유령이 빤히 쳐다보는 것을 느끼고 말을 멈추었다.

"무슨 일이지?" 유령이 물었다.

"아무것도 아닙니다." 스크루지가 말했다.

p.81 "뭔가 있는 것 같은데?" 유령이 말을 이었다.

"아니에요." 스크루지가 말했다. "지금 당장 제 서기에게 뭐라고 말을 해 줄 수 있다면 좋을 텐데요. 그뿐이에요."

스크루지의 어린 자아는 잘 자라고 말하며 등불의 불빛을 낮췄다. 스크루지와 유령은 다시 허공에 나란히 서 있었다.

"내게 주어진 시간이 줄어드는군." 유령이 말했다. "서둘러!"

이 말은 스크루지에게 한 말도, 혹은 그가 볼 수 있는 누군가에게 한 말도 아니었지만, 모든 것이 즉시 바뀌었다. 또 다시 스크루지는 자신의 모습을 보았다. 그는 이제 나이가 더 들어 있었다. 그는 이제 성인이었다. 그의 얼굴에 깊은 주름이나 검버섯은 없었다. 하지만 그의 얼굴에는 탐욕의 징조가 정말로 있었다. 그의 눈에는 간절히 원하고 탐욕스러운 무언가가 있었다. p.82 그의 눈은 그의 마음에 돈에 대한 열정이 뿌리를 내리고 자라나는 이기심의 나무의 그림자를 드리웠다는 것을 보여 주었다.

스크루지는 혼자가 아니었고, 검은 옷을 입은 예쁜 젊은 여자 옆에 앉아 있었다. 그녀의 눈에는 눈물이 고여 있었는데, 그 눈물은 과거의 크리스마스 유령에게서 뿜어져 나온 빛 속에서 반짝거렸다.

"그것은 전혀 중요하지 않아요." 그녀가 부드럽게 말했다. "당신에게는 아주 중요하지 않아요. 다른 무언가가 저를 대신해 왔어요. 만약 그것이 제가 애써 왔듯이 장차 당신을 기운 나게 하고 위안을 줄 수 있다면, 저는 슬퍼할 합당한 이유가 하나도 없어요."

"무엇이 당신을 대신했다는 거지?" 스크루지가 물었다.

"황금 우상이요." 그녀가 대답했다.

"이 이야기는 터무니없군!" 스크루지가 말했다. "당신이 가난하다는 것이 얼마나 힘든 것인지 알아? 부자가 되고 싶은 것에는 아무것도 잘못된 것이 없어!"

"당신은 세상을 너무 많이 두려워해요." 그녀가 다정하게 말했다. "당신의 모든 다른 소망들은 부자가 되겠다는 소망으로 합체되어 왔어요. p.83 저는 당신이 가지고 있는 더 고귀한 소망이 탐욕만 남을 때까지 하나씩 죽어 가는 것을 보았어요."

"그게 어때서?" 스크루지가 말했다. "나는 훨씬 더 현명해졌어, 그렇지 않아? 당신을 향한 내 마음은 변하지 않아."

그녀는 고개를 저었다.

"내가 변한다고?" 스크루지가 물었다.

"우리의 관계는 오래된 관계예요." 그녀가 말했다. "상황이 변하기 전까지는 그렇게 되기에는 우리 둘 다 가난하고 그래도 행복했던 때에 그것이 만들어졌지요. 우리는 참을성 있게 고된 일을 함으로써 우리의 물질적인 재산을 늘릴 수 있었어요. 당신은 변하고 있어요. 우리의 관계가 형성되었을 때, 당신은 다른 사람이었어요."

"나는 어린아이였어." 스크루지가 참지 못하고 말했다.

"당신도 마음속 깊은 곳에서는 당신이 변한 것을 알고 있잖아요." 그녀가 말했다. p.84 "저는 확신해요. 우리가 한마음이었을 때 우리를 행복하게 만든 것들이 이제 우리를 행복하게 해 주지 않을 거예요. 우리는 다시 다른 마음을 가지고 있어요. 제가 얼마나 자주 그리고 얼마나 예민하게 이에 대해 생각해 왔는지는 말하지 않겠어요. 하지만 저는 그 일에 대해 생각해 왔고 지금은 당신을 보내드릴 때예요."

"내가 나를 놓아 달라고 부탁한 적이 있었소?" 스크루지가 물었다.

"말로는 안 했죠." 그녀가 말했다. "한 번도요."

"그럼 무엇으로 그랬다는 거야?" 스크루지가 물었다.

"당신은 변한 성격, 변한 마음, 또 다른 삶의 분위기, 또 다른 희망으로 제게 부탁했어요." 그녀가 스크루지를 뚫어지게 바라보며 말했다. "이제 당신은 제 사랑이 필요 없어요. 그것은 이제 당신에게 중요하지 않죠. 만약 우리가 몇 년 전에 우리의 관계를 시작하지 않았다면, 말해 보세요, 당신은 지금 저를 찾아내어 저와 결혼하려고 애쓰실 거예요? 아, 아닐 거예요!"

"그렇게 생각하면 안 되지!" 스크루지가 소리쳤다. p.85 비록 그녀의 말에 동의하고 싶지는 않았지만, 그의 일부는 그것이 사실이라는 것을 알았다.

"할 수만 있다면 기꺼이 달리 생각하고 싶어요." 그녀가 말했다. "하느님께 맹세코요! 이와 같은 진실을 알게 되었을 때 저는 그것이 분명 얼마나 강력할지 알아요. 저는 그것을 잊을 수 없어요. 하지만 오늘이든 내일이든 어제든 당신이 자유의 몸이라면, 당신이 가난한 여자를 선택할 것이라고 제가 어떻게 믿을 수 있겠어요? 당신에게 돈 한 푼 가지고 오지 않을 여자를 당신이 왜 선택하겠어요? 만약 당신이 그 여자를 정말로 선택한다면, 당신이 얼마나 그 일을 후회할지 저는 알아요. 만약 당신이 오늘 저를 만났다면 당신은 저를 원하지 않았을 거라는 것을 저는 알아요. 그러니까 저는 당신을 보내 드릴 거예요. 저는 예전의 당신을 사랑하기 때문에 진심으로 당신을 보내 드리는 거예요."

스크루지가 막 말을 하려고 했으나, 여자는 스크루지에게서 고개를 돌리고 다시 말을 시작했다.

p.86 "당신은 이 일 때문에 고통스러울지도 몰라요." 그녀가 말했다. "제 일부는 좋은 추억 때문에 당신이 정말로 기분이 언짢기를 바라요. 당신은 잠시 동안만 기분이 언짢을 뿐일 거예요. 그런 다음 당신은 우리가 함께 한 시간이 어리석은 꿈이었다고 생각할 거예요. 당신이 선택해 온 삶을 살면서 당신이 행복하기를 바랄게요."

그녀는 스크루지를 떠났고, 그들은 헤어졌다.

"유령님!" 스크루지가 말했다. "더 이상 보여 주지 마세요! 나를 집으로 데려다주세요. 왜 나를 고문하는 것을 즐기십니까?"

"환영이 하나 더 있다!" 유령이 소리쳤다.

"더 이상은 싫어요!" 스크루지가 외쳤다. "더 이상은 싫어요. 나는 그것을 보고 싶지 않아요. 나에게 더 이상 보여 주지 마세요!"

하지만 유령은 스크루지의 양팔을 잡고 억지로 다음에 벌어지는 일을 지켜보게 했다.

그들은 또 다른 장소, 아주 크거나 예쁘지는 않지만 편안함이 한껏 느껴지는 어떤 방에 있었다. p.87 겨울 난롯가 근처에는 아름다운 어린 소녀가 앉아 있었다. 그녀는 스크루지를 떠났던 젊은 여자와 아주 많이 닮아 보였다. 맞은편에 앉아 있는 나이 든 여자를 보고 나서야 스크루지는 비로소 어린 소녀가 그녀의 딸이라는 것을 깨달았다. 스크루지가 셀 수도 없을 만큼 아이들이 많은 탓에 이 방 안의 소음은 대단히 요란했다. 그 아이들은 소리 지르고 장난 치고 점프하면서 뛰어다녔다.

너무 시끄러웠지만, 아무도 상관하지 않는 것 같았다. 그 대신에 어머니와 딸은 웃고 그 상황을 아주 많이 즐겼다. 딸은 아이들과 함께 놀기 시작했다. 아이들은 행복하게 어머니에게 덤비고 어머니와 함께 놀았다. 아이들은 어머니를 곯리고 팔을 어머니의 허리에 둘렀다.

그때 문가에서 노크 소리가 들렸고, 즉시 모든 아이들이 문으로 달려가 아버지를 맞았는데, 아이들의 아버지는 크리스마스 장난감과 선물들을 든 또 한 명의 남자와 함께 들어왔다. p.88 아이들은 소리를 지르고 가엾은 무방비 상태의 남자에게 뛰어오르기 시작했다! 아이들은 의자에 올라가고 아버지의 주머니에 손을 찔러 넣었다. 아이들은 사탕과 장난감들을 종이봉투에서 꺼냈다. 아이들은 목에 손을 둘러 아버지를 껴안고 아버지의 등을 때리고, 아버지의 다리를 걷어찼다!

아이들은 각각의 꾸러미를 열며 경탄과 기쁨으로 소리쳤다! 갑자기 누군가가 아기가 인형의 프라이팬을 먹었다고 소리쳤다. 그들은 아기가 그것을 자기 입에 넣은 것과 그것이 사라진 것을 알았다! 프라이팬이 다른 어딘가에 있는 것을 발견했을 때 모두는 기분이 나아졌다! 기쁨과 행복이 있었다! 그들은 자신들이 얼마나 행복한지 묘사할 수가 없었다. 오랜 시간이 걸렸지만, 마침내 아이들은 진정하고 다시 조용해졌다. p.89 그날 밤 늦게, 그들은 잠자리에 들었다.

그리고 이제 스크루지는 전보다 더 자세히 관찰했다. 자기 딸이 다정하게 몸을 기대 있는 동안 아버지는 그 아이와 그 아이의 어머니와 함께 앉았다. 바로 그 순간, 스크루지는 이 우아하고 특별하며 흥미로운 소녀가 이 남자 대신 자신을 아버지라고 불렀을 수도 있었겠다는 것을 깨달았다. 소녀는 겨울을 봄처럼 느끼도록 해 줄 수 있었을 것이었다. 스크루지의 마음은 몹시 무거워졌다.

"여보, 내가 오늘 오후에 당신의 옛 친구 한 명을 보았소." 남편이 미소를 짓고 자기 아내에게 몸을 돌리며 말했다.

"그게 누구였는데요?" 아내가 물었다.

"맞혀 보구려!" 남편이 말했다.

"제가 어떻게요?" 남편이 웃자 아내도 웃으며 말했다. "스크루지 씨로군요."

p.90 "스크루지 씨였소." 남편이 말했다. "나는 그 사람의 사무실 창문을 지나갔소. 창문이 닫혀 있지 않았고, 그 사람이 안에서 촛불을 켜 놓고

있어서 그를 볼 수 있었다오. 듣자니 그의 동업자는 죽은 거나 거의 마찬가지라고 하더군. 거기에 그가 혼자 앉아 있었소. 세상에서 완전히 혼자였다고 나는 믿소."

"유령님!" 스크루지가 갈라진 목소리로 말했다. "나를 이곳에서 꺼내 주세요."

"내가 말했듯이 이것들은 지금까지 존재해 온 것들의 환영이다." 유령이 말했다. "과거가 그랬으니 그렇게 보이는 것이다. 나에게 화내지 마라!"

"나를 데려다주세요!" 스크루지가 소리쳤다. "나는 저 상황을 지켜볼 수가 없어요."

스크루지는 유령에게 몸을 돌렸다. 유령의 얼굴을 쳐다보았을 때, 스크루지는 유령의 얼굴에서 자신이 방금 보았던 모든 사람들의 얼굴들을 보았다.

"나를 놔 줘!" 스크루지가 소리쳤다. "나를 놀려보내줘. 더 이상 너에게 붙어 다니지 마."

유령은 스크루지가 몸부림을 치는 동안 그를 꼭 잡고 있었다. 스크루지가 하는 행동은 아무것도 유령을 괴롭히지 않는 것 같았다. p.91 유령은 스크루지를 온화하게 바라보기만 했다. 스크루지는 유령이 내뿜는 빛이 높고 밝게 타오르고 있는 것을 보았다. 스크루지는 그 빛이 자기에게 이 모든 것들을 보여 주고 있는 것임을 깨달았다. 스크루지는 모자를 잡고 갑자기 모자를 유령의 머리 위에 놓고 내리눌렀다.

모자가 그의 몸 전체를 덮을 정도로 유령은 모자 아래에서 크기가 줄어들었다. 비록 스크루지가 온 힘을 다해 눌렀지만, 그 빛을 숨길 수는 없었다. 빛은 모자 아래에서 끊이지 않는 빛의 홍수를 이루어 땅바닥으로 흘러나왔다.

스크루지는 자신이 몹시 피곤하다는 것과 자신이 자신의 침실에 있다는 것을 깨달았다. 스크루지는 모자를 마지막으로 짓눌렀다. 그러고 나서 스크루지는 긴장이 풀려 간신히 침대에 들 시간을 가졌고 비로소 깊은 잠에 빠졌다.

세 유령들 중 두 번째 유령

p.92 드르렁드르렁 요란하게 코를 골던 도중에 깨어나 생각들을 하나

로 모으기 위해 일어나 침대에 앉은 스크루지는 다음 유령이 곧 올 것이라는 것을 알았다. 스크루지는 자신에게 올 것으로 예상되는 두 번째 유령을 맞이하기 위해 안성맞춤인 시각에 잠에서 깼다고 생각했다.

p.93 유령이 자신의 커튼 중 어느 것을 열지 궁금해 하기 시작했을 때 스크루지는 거북할 정도로 오싹해졌다. 스크루지는 커튼을 모두 열어 두어야겠다고 마음먹었다. 스크루지는 유령을 보자마자 그를 맞이하고 싶었다. 스크루지는 놀라거나 초조해하고 싶지 않았다.

아주 느긋하고 참을성이 많은 사람들이 조금 있다. 그들은 모든 종류의 이상한 것들을 볼 수 있지만 상관하지 않는다. 스크루지는 그렇게 참을성이 있지는 않았으나, 이제 그의 마음은 약간 변했다. 그날 밤 그 순간에, 스크루지는 설령 코뿔소에 올라탄 아기만큼 이상한 것일지라도 무엇이든 볼 준비가 되어 있었다.

이제 거의 어떤 것이든 맞이할 준비가 되어 있었기 때문에, 스크루지는 아무것도 맞이할 것이 없는 것에 대해서는 준비가 전혀 되어 있지 않았다. 그래서 시계가 1시를 치고 어떠한 형상도 나타나지 않았을 때, 스크루지는 벌벌 떨기 시작했다. 5분, 10분, 15분이 지나갔지만, 아무것도 오지 않았다. p.94 이러는 내내 스크루지는 침대에 누워 있었다.

시계가 그 다음 시각을 쳤을 때 스크루지의 방 안으로 들어온 붉은 빛은 열두 명의 유령들보다도 깜짝 놀라게 하는 것이었다. 스크루지는 그 상황을 이해하기에는 무기력했다. 스크루지는 자신도 모르게 갑자기 자신이 발화할지도 모른다고 두려워하기 시작했다.

하지만 마침내 스크루지는 이 희미한 빛이 옆방에서 나오고 있을지도 모른다고 생각하기 시작했다. 더욱 자세히 보았을 때, 스크루지는 그 빛이 그곳으로부터 나오는 것 같다는 것을 깨달았다. 이러한 생각이 사실이라고 결론 내렸을 때, 스크루지는 조용히 일어나 슬리퍼를 신고 그곳으로 걸어갔다.

스크루지의 손이 문에 닿는 순간, 낯선 목소리가 스크루지의 이름을 부르고 들어오라고 말했다. 스크루지는 안으로 들어갔다.

그것은 스크루지 자신의 방이었다. 그 점에 관해서는 의심의 여지가 없었다. 하지만 놀라운 변화가 있었다. 벽과 천장이 살아 있는 초록 식물들로 장식되어 있었다. p.95 방은 완벽한 정원처럼 보였다. 정원의 모든 부분에서 선명하게 빛나는 베리들이 자랐다. 싱싱한 서양호랑가시나무, 겨우살이,

그리고 담쟁이덩굴의 잎들은 마치 아주 많은 작은 거울들이 그 위로 빛을 흩뜨리는 것처럼 빛을 다시 반사했다. 아주 커다랗게 피운 불이 벽난로 안에서 으르렁거렸다. 벽난로는 말리나 스크루지가 그 집에 살았던 오래 전 이후로 그처럼 큰 불을 피운 적이 없었다.

칠면조고기, 거위고기, 사슴고기, 닭고기, 소고기, 돼지고기, 그리고 긴 줄의 소시지들이 왕의 옥좌 모양으로 바닥에 쌓여 있었다. 그 꼭대기에는 고기 파이, 자두 푸딩, 굴을 담은 통들, 그리고 빨갛게 익은 밤들이 있었다. 또한 사과, 즙이 많은 오렌지, 맛있는 배, 아주 커다란 케이크, 펀치 그릇들이 있었다. **p.96** 방 전체에는 맛있는 음식 냄새가 났다.

보기에 경이롭고 유쾌한 거인이 이 의자에 앉아 있었다. 거인은 뿔 모양으로 타오르는 횃불을 높이 들고 있었다. 스크루지가 방으로 들어갈 때 빛이 스크루지에게 떨어졌다.

"들어와!" 유령이 소리쳤다. "더 가까이 와, 이 사람아!"

스크루지는 쭈뼛쭈뼛 안으로 들어가 이 유령에게 고개를 숙였다. 그는 예전의 완고한 스크루지가 아니었으며, 유령의 눈이 밝고 인자했음에도 불구하고 스크루지는 그 눈과 마주치기를 싫어했다.

"나는 현재의 크리스마스 유령이다." 유령이 말했다. "나를 봐!"

스크루지는 마치 그 유령이 왕이라도 되는 양 유령을 쳐다보았다. 유령은 흰 모피가 달린 단순한 초록색 로브를 입고 있었다. 이 옷은 유령의 몸에 아주 느슨하게 걸쳐져 있어서 그의 튼튼한 가슴의 맨살이 드러났다. 긴 옷 맨 밑의 유령의 발 역시 맨발이었다. **p.97** 유령은 머리 위에 반짝이는 은박지 장식이 달려 있는 서양호랑가시나무 화관을 쓰고 있었다. 유령의 짙은 갈색 고수머리는 길고 제멋대로 흩어져 있었다. 유령의 얼굴은 온화했다. 유령의 반짝이는 눈, 활짝 편 손, 명랑한 목소리, 그리고 그의 유쾌한 태도 모두 자유분방했다. 허리에는 검집을 차고 있었지만, 검은 없고 비어 있었다.

"나 같은 유령은 전에 한 번도 본 적이 없는 모양이군!" 유령이 소리쳤다.

"한 번도 없어요." 스크루지가 대답했다.

"내 형제들과 걸어본 적이 한 번도 없나?" 유령이 말을 이었다. "알겠지만 나는 아주 어린 편인데."

"나는 그런 적이 없는 것 같아요." 스크루지가 말했다. "나는 그런 적이 없는 것 같아요. 형제가 많으신가요, 유령님?"

"1,800명도 더 되지." 유령이 말했다.

p.98 "부양하기에는 거대한 가족이군요!" 스크루지가 짜증내며 말했다.

현재의 크리스마스 유령이 일어섰다.

"유령님, 나를 원하시는 어디로든 데려가 주세요." 스크루지가 말했다. "어젯밤에 유령님이 나에게 길을 떠나게 했고, 이제는 이해가 되는 교훈을 배웠습니다. 오늘 밤 만약 나에게 가르쳐 주실 무언가가 있으시다면 내가 그것을 배우게 해 주세요."

"내 옷을 만져라!" 유령이 말했다.

스크루지는 자신이 들은 대로 하고 유령의 옷을 꽉 잡았다.

서양호랑가시나무, 겨우살이, 붉은 베리, 담쟁이덩굴, 칠면조고기, 거위고기, 닭고기, 소고기, 돼지고기, 소시지, 굴, 파이, 푸딩, 과일, 그리고 펀치가 모두 즉시 사라졌다. 방도, 불도, 붉은 빛도, 밤 시간도 사라졌고, 그들은 크리스마스 아침에 도시의 거리에 서 있었다. 전날 밤 눈이 와서 사람들이 그들의 집에서 눈을 쓸며 시끄럽게 떠들었다. p.99 눈이 집에서 떨어지는 것을 보는 것은 아이들을 즐겁게 했다.

지붕 위의 포근한 하얀 눈 더미와 땅 위의 더러운 눈 때문에 그 집 정면은 새까매 보였으며, 창문들은 더 까매 보였다. 마차들의 바퀴와 말들이 눈을 더럽게 만들고 누런 눈과 진흙으로 된 복잡한 무늬를 만들었다. 하늘은 우중충했고, 가장 길이가 짧은 길들에는 탁한 안개가 자욱했으며 반은 눈이 녹고 반은 꽁꽁 얼어 있었다. 날씨에서도 혹은 마을에서도 아주 유쾌한 것은 아무것도 없었으나, 마치 아름다운 화창한 날인 것처럼 활기찬 분위기가 있었다.

집 꼭대기에서 눈을 삽으로 치우는 사람들은 즐거워했다. 그들은 서로에게 소리를 치고 눈덩이를 던지고 자기들이 누군가를 맞추거나 맞추지 못하면 즐겁게 웃었다. p.100 닭고기를 파는 가게들은 여전히 반쯤은 열려 있었고, 과일 가게들은 눈 속에서 밝고 아름답게 보였다. 쾌활한 노신사의 외투 모양처럼 생긴 커다랗고 둥근 모양의 밤을 담은 바구니들이 있었다. 그것들은 현관문 앞에 놓여 있거나 거리로 흘러 넘쳐 있었다. 뚱뚱한 스페인 수도사처럼 반짝이는, 표면이 불그스름한 스페인 양파가 있었다.

융성한 피라미드 모양으로 무리를 지어 높이 쌓아 놓은 배와 사과들이 있었다. 가게에 주렁주렁 매달린 포도송이들이 있었다. 사람들이 지나갈 때 그들의 입에는 침이 고였다. 사람들에게 그 옛날의 숲 속의 산책로와 갈색 나뭇잎 속에서 놀던 일을 생각나게 하는 냄새가 났다. 심지어는 선명한 색깔의 오렌지와 레몬들도 있었다. 그것들은 아주 맛있게 보여서 사람들로 하여금 종이봉투에 담아 집으로 가지고 가서 저녁 식사 후에 그것들을 먹고 싶게 만들었다.

p.101 이 선명한 색깔의 과일들 사이에서 그릇에 담긴 채 놓여 있는 금색과 은색의 물고기들은 그날이 특별한 날이라는 것을 아는 듯했다. 그 물고기들은 느릿느릿한 흥분 상태로 빙글빙글 맴을 돌며 헤엄쳤다. 하지만 가 봐야 할 가장 근사한 장소는 식품점이었다! 깡통과 종이 소리들이 유쾌한 음악을 만들어 냈다.

차와 커피가 섞인 냄새는 아주 좋았다. 건포도들은 아주 맛있었고, 아몬드는 아주 하얗고, 계피 막대들은 아주 길고 곧았다. 다른 양념들 또한 맛있어 보였다. 설탕에 절인 과일들은 달콤한 액상 설탕으로 뒤덮여 있었다. 무화과는 촉촉했고, 프랑스산 자두는 달곰씁쓸했다.

p.102 그 특별한 날 때문에 고객들은 모두 몹시도 허둥대고 몹시도 열성적이었다. 그들은 문간에서 서로 부딪쳤고, 자신들의 바구니를 와장창 부수었고, 계산대 위에 자신들이 산 물건들을 놓고 갔다. 그러고 나서는 그것들을 가지러 다시 달려왔다. 그들은 행복해하며 수많은 작은 실수들을 저질렀다. 한편 식품점에서 일하는 사람들은 특히 깔끔하고 전문적으로 보였다.

하지만 곧 종들이 울렸고 착한 사람들을 모두 교회와 예배당으로 불렀다. 그들은 가장 좋은 옷을 입고 가장 행복한 얼굴로 길을 나서 거리 여기저기로 몰려들었다. 동시에 사람들은 그들의 저녁 식사를 들고 나와 빵가게로 향했다.

이 사람들은 유령을 무척 흥미롭게 해 준 것 같았다. 횃불을 가지고 유령은 그들의 음식 위에 무언가를 흩뿌렸다. 그리고 그것은 아주 특별한 종류의 횃불이었다. 한두 번 서로를 밀치던 일부 사람들 사이에서 말다툼이 있었을 때, 유령은 횃불에서 몇 방울의 물을 사람들 위로 흘렸다. p.103 그러자 그들은 갑자기 다시 행복해졌다. 그들은 크리스마스에 말다툼을 하는 것은 부끄러운 일이라고 말했다.

때마침 종소리가 멈추었고, 제빵사들은 가게 문을 닫았다. 하지만 음식은 아직 요리 중이었고 오븐 주변의 눈은 녹고 있었다.

"유령님의 횃불에서 흩뿌린 것에는 특별한 맛이 있나요?" 스크루지가 물었다.

"있지." 유령이 말했다. "나만의 맛이야."

"그 맛이 이 날에는 어떤 종류의 저녁 식사에라도 적용되나요?" 스크루지가 물었다.

"정성껏 제공된 저녁 식사라면 어떤 것에도 적용될 거야." 유령이 대답했다. "특히 그것이 가난한 사람들에게 제공된다면 말이야."

p.104 "왜 가난한 사람에게 가장 잘 적용되지요?" 스크루지가 물었다.

"그 사람이 그 맛을 가장 필요로 하니까." 유령이 말했다.

"유령님, 왜 유령님이 사람들에게 상황을 즐길 날들을 더 적게 주려고 하시는지 궁금하군요." 스크루지가 말했다.

"내가!" 유령이 외쳤다.

"유령님은 매주 일요일마다 그들의 식사를 가져가시잖아요." 스크루지가 말했다. "그리고 그날은 그들이 일하지 않는 유일한 날이고요! 사실 아닌가요?"

"내가!" 유령이 소리쳤다.

"유령님이 일요일에는 이 가게들을 닫으시잖아요?" 스크루지가 말했다. "그러면 그들은 쉬지도 혹은 즐거움을 얻지도 못하지요."

"내가 가게 문을 닫는다고!" 유령이 소리쳤다.

"제가 틀린 거라면 용서해 주세요." 스크루지가 말했다. "문을 닫는 것이 유령님의 이름 혹은 적어도 유령님의 가족 이름으로 이루어져 왔거든요."

"우리의 이름으로 사악하고 교만하고 이기적인 일들을 하는 몇몇 사람들이 있어." 유령이 말했다. p.105 "그들은 우리들에게는 낯선 사람들이야. 그것을 명심하고, 우리가 아닌 그들에게 화를 내도록 해."

스크루지는 그러겠다고 약속했고, 그들은 계속해서 사람들 눈에 보이지 않는 채로 마을의 외곽으로 갔다. 설사 유령의 체구가 거대하다고 하더라도 스크루지는 그가 어느 장소에나 쉽게 스스로를 끼워 맞춘다는 것을 깨달았다. 유령은 낮은 지붕 아래에서도 높은 천장이 달린 홀에 서 있을 수 있는 것만큼이나 아주 우아하게 서 있었다.

아마도 유령은 자신의 힘을 보여 주고 싶어 하거나 가난한 사람들에게 동정심을 느낀 듯했다. 유령은 스크루지를 곧장 스크루지의 서기의 집으로 안내했다. 유령은 자신의 옷을 잡고 있는 스크루지를 실내로 데려갔다. 현관 앞에서 유령은 미소를 짓고 자신의 횃불에서 물을 뿌려 밥 크래칫의 집을 축복해 주려고 멈추어 섰다. 그 점에 대해 생각해 보라! 밥이 아주 가난하기는 했지만, 크리스마스 유령이 그의 집을 축복해 주었다니!

p.106 그런 다음 싸구려 옷을 입은 크래칫의 아내인 크래칫 부인이 일어났다. 크래칫 부인의 드레스는 예쁜 크리스마스 리본들로 뒤덮여 있었다. 크래칫 부인은 역시 리본을 달고 있는 둘째 딸 벨린다 크래칫의 도움을 받아 그 드레스를 만들었다. 장남인 피터 크래칫은 자신의 포크를 감자 냄비 안으로 집어넣었다. 피터는 너무 큰 셔츠를 입고 있었다. 하지만 그의 아버지가 그 옷을 크리스마스 선물로 피터에게 준 터였다. 아버지는 피터가 자신의 새로운 패션을 자랑하기 위해 공원에 갈 수 있기를 바랐다.

그리고 이제 두 명의 어린 크래칫 남매가 자기들이 거위고기 냄새를 맡았다고 소리를 지르며 달려 들어왔다. 그들은 그 고기를 먹고 싶어 했다. 샐비어와 양파 냄새가 아주 좋아서 이 어린 크래칫 남매는 식탁 주위에서 춤을 추었다. 그들은 장남인 피터 크래칫을 칭찬하고 그를 미남이라고 불렀다. 그들이 춤을 추는 동안 피터는 미소를 짓고 냄비 안에 있는 감자들을 계속해서 끓였다.

p.107 "아버지는 어디에 계시니?" 크래칫 부인이 말했다. "그리고 막내 팀도! 그리고 마사는 지난 크리스마스 때 30분씩 늦지는 않았는데!"

"마사가 왔어요, 어머니!" 아가씨가 말했고, 그녀는 말을 하는 동안 모습을 드러냈다.

"마사 누나가 왔어요, 어머니!" 두 명의 어린 크래칫 남매가 소리쳤다. "만세! 거위고기가 있어, 마사!"

"어머나, 저런, 내 사랑하는 딸아, 많이 늦었구나!" 열두 번이나 딸에게 입을 맞추고 열심히 딸의 외투와 모자를 벗겨 주며 크래칫 부인이 말했다.

"어젯밤에는 끝내야 할 일이 많았어요." 마사가 대답했다. "그리고 오늘 아침에는 눈을 치워야 했어요, 어머니!"

"그래, 신경 쓰지 마라!" 크래칫 부인이 말했다. "네가 온 것만 해도 기쁘구나. 난롯불 앞에 앉아라, 얘야. 그리고 몸을 녹이렴. p.108 주님의 축복이 함께 하기를!"

"아니, 안 돼!" 두 명의 어린 크래칫 남매가 소리쳤다. "아버지가 오고 계셔. 숨어, 마사, 숨으라고!"

그래서 마사는 몸을 숨겼고, 아버지인 조그만 체구의 밥은 담요를 자신의 마른 몸에 두르고 들어왔다. 밥은 자신의 허름한 옷을 크리스마스답시고 근사하게 보이게 하려고 세탁해 두려고 애썼었다. 막내 팀은 밥의 어깨 위에 앉아 있었다. 불쌍한 막내 팀, 그 아이는 목발 없이는 걸을 수 없었다!

"이런, 우리 마사는 어디에 있지?" 밥 크래칫이 두리번거리며 외쳤다.

"안 올 거예요." 크래칫 부인이 말했다.

"안 올 거라고!" 갑자기 슬픈 표정을 지으며 밥이 말했다. 밥은 팀을 등에 업고 교회에서 집까지 아주 빨리 달려 온 것이었다. "크리스마스에 오지 않을 거라고!"

장난으로라도 마사는 밥이 실망하는 것을 보는 것을 좋아하지 않았다. 그래서 마사는 벽장 문 뒤에서 일찍 나와 밥의 품 안으로 달려들었다. p.109 두 명의 어린 크래칫 남매는 막내 팀을 데리고 가서 목욕을 할 수 있도록 옷을 벗겨 주었다.

"그런데 막내 팀은 교회에서 어땠어요?" 밥이 자기 딸을 행복하게 껴안아 줄 때 크래칫 부인이 물었다.

"팀은 아주 얌전했어." 밥이 말했다. "웬일인지 팀은 생각이 깊어지고, 아주 오래 혼자 앉아서 들어본 적이 없는 너무나 이상한 생각을 하는 거야. 집에 오면서 팀은 자기가 절름발이니까 사람들이 교회에서 자기를 보았으면 좋겠다고 하더군. 그렇게 해서 예수님이 어떻게 장님들을 보게 하고 절름발이들을 걷게 하셨는지 그들에게 기억나게 해 주고 싶었다는 거야."

식구들에게 이 이야기를 해 줄 때 밥의 목소리는 떨렸고 막내 팀이 점점 튼튼해지고 건강해지고 있다고 말할 때는 더욱 떨렸다. p.110 그들은 마룻바닥에서 나는 팀의 목발 소리와 막내 팀이 그의 형과 누나와 함께 돌아오는 소리를 들었다. 그들은 팀을 난롯불 앞에 있는 의자 위에 앉혔다. 밥은 진과 레몬을 물 주전자 속에 넣어 무언가 뜨거운 것을 만들었고, 그것을 빙글빙글 젓고서는 난로 위에 두어 부글부글 끓였다. 장남 피터와 두 명의 어린 크래칫 남매는 거위고기를 가지러 갔다. 그들은 곧 그것을 가지고 돌아왔다.

거위고기를 보았을 때 그들 모두는 아주 신이 났다. 크래칫 부인은 육즙을 만들었는데, 그것은 여전히 뜨거웠다. 장남인 피터는 열심히 감자를 으깨었다. 벨린다는 사과 소스를 달게 만들었다. 마사는 요리용 철판을 닦았다. 밥은 막내 팀을 식탁의 작은 구석, 자기 옆에 앉혔다.

두 명의 어린 크래칫 남매는 모두를 위해 의자를 마련했고, 자기들의 의자도 잊지 않았다. 마침내 그들은 숟가락을 자기들 입 안으로 밀어 넣었다. 그들은 다른 사람들이 거위고기를 모두 먹어 치우는 것을 원하지 않았다. 마침내 접시들이 음식으로 채워지고, 모두는 기도를 했다.

p.111 숨죽인 기다림이 이어졌고, 그때 크래칫 부인은 천천히 칼을 쳐다보며 거위고기를 자를 준비를 했다. 크래칫 부인이 거위고기를 잘랐을 때 안에서 내용물이 쏟아져 나왔다. 모두가 식탁 주위에 둘러앉아 기쁨의 미소를 지었다. 심지어는 두 명의 어린 크래칫 남매로 인해 덩달아 신이 난 막내 팀까지 자신의 칼을 가지고 식탁을 두드렸으며 조그맣게나마 만세를 외쳤다!

그런 거위고기는 없었다. 밥은 그렇게 요리된 거위가 있다는 것이 믿겨지지 않는다고 말했다. 거위고기의 맛, 크기, 싼값은 모두가 칭찬하는 것이었다. 사과 소스와 으깬 감자와 함께, 거위고기는 가족 전체에게는 훌륭한 저녁 식사였다.

p.112 정말로, 크래칫 부인이 대단히 기쁘게 말한 바와 같이 그들은 그 식사를 끝낼 수가 없었다. 그러나 모두들 충분히 먹었다. 크래칫가의 가장 어린 아이들은 샐비어와 양파를 몇 부스러기나 먹어 치웠다! 하지만 이제 접시들은 벨린다에 의해 치워지고 있었다. 크래칫 부인은 푸딩을 꺼내 식탁으로 가지고 오려고 혼자 방을 떠났다. 크래칫 부인은 아주 긴장되었다!

푸딩이 충분히 익지 않았으면 어쩌지? 너무 많이 익혀졌으면 어쩌지? 누군가가 푸딩을 훔쳤다면 어쩌지? 온갖 종류의 무서운 생각이 났다. 푸딩은 아주 뜨거웠다. 푸딩이 오븐 밖으로 꺼내졌다. 30초 후에 크래칫 부인은 의기양양하게 미소를 지으며 푸딩을 가지고 들어왔다. 푸딩은 아주 단단했다. 크리스마스 서양호랑가시나무가 맨 위에 꽂혀 있었다.

"오, 근사한 푸딩이구려!" 밥 크래칫이 말했다.

밥은 그 푸딩이 그들의 결혼 이후 크래칫 부인이 이룬 가장 대단한 성공작이라고 생각했다. 크래칫 부인은 이제 자기는 더 이상 긴장되지 않으니까 자기가 얼마나 걱정했었는지 말할 수 있다고 말했다. p.113 모두가 그에 관해 무언가 해 줄 말이 있기는 했으나, 그것이 대가족의 규모에 어울리기에는 완전히 작은 푸딩이라고 말하거나 생각하는 사람은 아무도 없었다. 크래칫가의 사람 중 누구라도 그러한 것을 넌지시 비추었다가는 얼굴을 붉혔을 것이었다.

마침내 저녁 식사가 모두 끝났고, 식탁보는 치워졌으며, 벽난로는 청소되었고, 불이 다시 붙여졌다. 주전자 안의 진을 섞은 레몬주스의 맛이 선보여졌는데, 그 맛은 완벽했다. 사과와 오렌지가 식탁 위에 놓였고 많은 밤이 불 위에 올려졌다. 그런 다음 크래칫가의 사람들은 모두 벽난로 주위로 모였다. 밥 크래칫의 팔꿈치는 그 가족이 가지고 있는 가장 좋은 유리컵들 옆에 있었다. 그 유리컵들 중 하나는 약간 이가 나갔다.

하지만 이 유리컵들은 황금 컵만큼이나 물 주전자에서 따른 뜨거운 음료를 잘 담아 내고 있었다. p.114 밤들이 불 위에서 요란하게 딱딱거리며 소리를 내는 동안, 밥은 활짝 미소를 지으며 그 음료를 대접했다.

"나의 사랑하는 가족들, 우리 모두에게 즐거운 크리스마스가 되기를!" 밥이 말했다. "주님이 우리를 축복해 주시기를!"

가족들 전부 그 말을 되풀이했다.

"우리 각자 모두에게 신의 은총이 가득하기를!" 마지막으로 막내 팀이 말했다.

막내 팀은 자신의 작은 의자 위에서 자기 아버지 쪽으로 아주 바짝 붙어 앉아 있었다. 밥은 그 아이를 정말 사랑한다는 듯이 막내 팀의 힘없는 작은 손을 잡았다. 밥은 막내 팀을 자기 옆에 계속 두고 싶어 했으며 그 아이를 잃을까 봐 두려워했다.

"유령님, 막내 팀이 살게 될지 저한테 말씀해 주세요." 스크루지가 전에는 느껴본 적이 없는 관심을 가지고 말했다.

"내 눈에는 저 구석에 빈 의자와 주인이 없는 목발이 보인다." 유령이 대답했다. "만약 미래의 유령에 의해 이 환영들이 바뀌지 않고 남아 있다면, 저 아이는 죽게 될 것이다."

p.115 "안 돼요, 안 돼." 스크루지가 말했다. "오, 안 돼요, 인자한 유령님! 사실이 아니라고 말씀해 주세요!"

"만약 미래의 유령에 의해 이 환영들이 바뀌지 않고 남아 있다면, 저 아이는 다음번 크리스마스를 보지 못할 거야." 유령이 말했다. "그렇게 되면 뭐가 어떻다는 거냐? 만약 그 아이가 죽을 것 같다면, 차라리 그러는 편이 더 낫다. 그런 식으로 인구는 줄어들 테니까. 사람들이 너무 많아, 맞지?"

자기가 하던 말을 유령에게 듣게 되어 스크루지는 고개를 떨어뜨렸다. 스크루지의 마음속에는 후회가 가득했다.

"만약 네가 인간일 뿐이라면, 네가 어떻게 누가 잉여 인간이고, 그런 잉여 인간이 어디에 있는지 선택할 수 있겠느냐?" 유령이 말했다. "어떤 사람은 살고 어떤 사람은 죽을 것인지 네가 결정하겠느냐? 네가 이 불쌍한 남자의 아이, 혹은 그 아이와 같은 사람들보다 조금이라도 나으냐? 신에게는 너도 나뭇잎 위에 있는 벌레 같을 뿐이야."

p.116 스크루지는 유령의 말에 고개를 숙였고, 부들부들 떨면서 땅을 내려다보았다. 하지만 자신의 이름을 들었을 때 스크루지는 재빨리 눈을 들었다.

"스크루지 씨!" 밥이 말했다. "이 진수성찬을 차릴 돈을 우리에게 주신 스크루지 씨를 위해 건배하겠습니다!"

"그래야 하고말고요!" 크래칫 부인이 얼굴이 붉어지며 외쳤다. "그분이 이곳에 있으면 좋겠어요. 제가 그분에 대해 정말로 어떻게 생각하는지 그 분한테 보여 주고 싶어요! 그 영감님이 각오가 되어 있으면 좋겠네요!"

"여보." 밥이 말했다. "크리스마스에 아이들 앞에서 그런 소리는 하지 말아요."

"크리스마스는 스크루지 씨 같은 그런 끔찍하고 냉혹하고 무정한 사람의 건강을 위해 건배하는 단 하루뿐인 날이죠." 크래칫 부인이 말했다. "당신은 그 영감님을 잘 알잖아요, 여보! 아무도 당신보다 더 그 양반을 잘 알지는 못해요, 가엾은 양반!"

"여보, 오늘은 크리스마스야." 밥이 말했다.

p.117 "당신을 위해서 건배를 하겠어요. 크리스마스니까요. 하지만 그 영감님을 위해서는 아니에요." 크래칫 부인이 말했다. "스크루지 영감님의 만수무강을 위해! 즐거운 크리스마스 보내시고 새해 복 많이 받으시기를! 그 영감님은 아주 즐겁고 아주 행복할 거예요. 틀림없어요!"

아이들은 크래칫 부인을 따라 건배했다. 그것이 그날 그들이 했던 일 중 하기 싫어했던 최초의 일이었다. 막내 팀은 모든 가족 중 마지막으로 건배를 했지만, 그것을 전혀 좋아하지 않았다. 스크루지는 그 가족에게 괴물이었다. 그에 관해 이야기하는 것만으로도 파티에 어두운 그림자가 드리워졌고, 그 그림자는 꼬박 5분 동안이나 머물렀다.

그 어두운 그림자가 지나간 후, 스크루지에 관해 다시는 말하지 않아도 되기 때문에 그들은 전보다 열 배는 더 즐거워했다. 밥 크래칫은 장남 피터를 위한 일자리를 어떻게 찾았는지 식구들에게 말해 주었다. 두 명의 어린 크래칫 남매는 피터가 직장인이 된다는 생각에 몹시 웃었다. **p.118** 피터 자신은 자기 돈을 어떻게 쓸 것인지 결정하려고 애쓰며 생각에 잠겨 불을 바라보았다.

그때 가난한 견습생인 마사가 식구들에게 자기가 어떤 종류의 일을 해야 하고 얼마나 많은 시간을 일하는지를 말해 주었다. 마사는 다음날 하루 종일 자고 싶어 했는데, 그날이 휴일이기 때문이었다. 또한 자신이 며칠 전에 백작 부인과 영주를 보게 된 경위에 대해서도 말해 주었다. 영주는 '키가 피터만하더라'라고 마사는 말했다. 이러는 동안 밤과 주전자가 식구들 사이를 몇 바퀴 돌았다. 그들은 눈 속을 헤매다 길을 잃어버린 아이에 대한 노래를 불렀다. 막내 팀은 아름다운 작은 목소리로 노래를 불렀다.

그들에게는 풍족한 것이 아무것도 없었다. 그들은 잘생긴 가족이 아니었다. 그들이 옷을 잘 입은 것도 아니었다. 그들의 신발은 젖어 있었고, 옷은 낡았으며, 피터는 종종 곤경에 빠졌다. **p.119** 하지만 그들은 행복하고, 감사하고, 서로에게 만족했으며, 크리스마스 때면 더 행복했다. 그들의 모습이 희미해질 때, 유령이 그들에게 마법을 뿌린 후 그들은 훨씬 더 행복해 보였다. 스크루지는 그들을, 특히 막내 팀을 끝까지 지켜보았다.

이때쯤 날이 점점 어두워지고 눈은 펑펑 내리고 있었다. 스크루지와 유령이 거리를 따라 걷고 있을 때, 부엌, 거실, 그리고 온갖 종류의 방에서 이글거리는 불의 밝기는 굉장했다. 불빛은 난로 앞에서 음식을 굽고 있는 요리용 철판과 함께 안락한 저녁 식사의 준비 모습을 보여 주었다.

창문들에는 추위와 어둠을 막기 위해 닫힐 채비가 되어 있는 짙은 붉은 색의 커튼이 달려 있었다. 집안의 모든 아이들은 그들의 결혼한 형제자매, 사촌, 삼촌, 숙모들을 만나 그들에게 먼저 인사를 하려고 눈 속으로 달려 나가고 있었다.

p.120 또 다른 집에서는 또 다른 무리의 환영들이 있었다. 모두 두건을 쓰고 털 장화를 신고 모두가 동시에 이야기하고 있는 예쁜 소녀들의 무리가 있었다. 그들은 아름답고 발갛게 달아오른 것처럼 보였다! 그들을 보는 총각은 누구라도 그들을 사랑하게 될 것이었다!

다른 사람들을 방문하는 사람들이 아주 많이 있어서, 집 안에서 그들이 오는 것을 기다리는 사람들이 있다는 것을 믿기가 힘들었다. 유령은 아주 행복했다! 유령은 손을 펴고 모두에게 축복과 행복을 주었다! 밤에 불을 켜는 남자, 그러니까 그날 저녁을 어딘가에서 보내려고 옷을 차려입은 점등원은 유령이 지나갈 때 큰 소리로 웃었다!

p.121 그리고 이제, 유령으로부터 경고도 하나 받지 못하고, 그들은 공터에 서 있었다. 그곳에는 마치 거인이라도 묻혀 있는 듯 커다란 돌덩이들

이 있었다. 물은 이상한 무늬를 만들며 얼어붙어 있었다. 이끼와 풀 외에는 아무것도 자라지 않았다. 서쪽으로 지는 해는 타는 듯한 붉은색으로 보였다. 해는 점점 더 아래로 지고 있었고, 어두운 밤의 짙은 음울함 속으로 사라졌다.

"이곳은 어떤 곳인가요?" 스크루지가 물었다.

"땅속 깊은 곳에서 일하는 광부들이 사는 곳이다." 유령이 대답했다. "하지만 그들은 나를 안다. 봐라!"

오두막집 창문에서 불빛이 반짝였고, 그들은 재빨리 그곳을 향해 달려갔다. 진흙과 돌로 만든 벽을 지나, 그들은 발갛게 타오르는 난롯불 주위에 앉아 있는 명랑한 일행을 발견했다. 나이가 아주 많은 남녀가 자신의 자녀들과 손자 손녀들, 심지어 증손자 증손녀들까지 함께 모두 명절 옷을 차려입고 있었다.

p.122 노인은 대체로 바람 소리보다 결코 크지 않은 목소리로 그들에게 크리스마스 노래를 불러 주고 있었다. 때때로 그들은 모두 합창에 참여했다. 노인은 다른 사람들이 자신과 함께 노래하는 것을 즐거워했고 훨씬 더 큰 소리로 노래했다.

유령은 이곳에서 오래 기다리지 않았지만 스크루지에게 자기 옷을 잡으라고 했다. 그들은 어디로 갈 것인가? 설마 바다는 아니겠지? 그들은 바다로 날아갔다. 뒤돌아보니 스크루지에게는 무섭게도 육지의 끝 부분과 그 뒤의 무시무시한 암벽들이 보였다. 암벽에 부딪히는 커다란 물소리 때문에 스크루지는 소리를 듣지 못했다.

바닷물이 거세게 일어나는 해안과 멀리 떨어진 무시무시한 암벽 위에 등대가 하나 세워져 있었다. 해초 조각들이 그 밑에 들러붙어 있고 커다란 바닷새들이 그 주변을 날았다.

p.123 하지만 이곳에서도 등대를 감시하는 두 남자가 불을 피웠다. 두꺼운 돌 벽 안의 구멍을 통해서 그 불은 무시무시한 바다 위로 밝은 빛줄기를 내보냈다. 자기들이 앉아 있는 조악한 탁자 위로 거칠어진 손을 마주 잡은 채, 그들은 서로에게 즐거운 크리스마스가 되기를 기원해 주었다. 그들 중 얼굴이 온통 상처투성이에다 흉터가 있는 나이가 더 많은 남자가 힘차게 부는 바람 같은 노래를 부르기 시작했다.

또 다시 유령은 배 한 척을 발견할 때까지 검고 요동치는 바다 위로 계속해서 날아갔다. 그들은 선장 옆에 섰다. 그 배에서 일하는 사람들은 피부가 검고, 유령 같은 모습이었다. 그러나 모든 사람들이 크리스마스 노래를 흥얼거리거나 크리스마스 생각을 했다.

p.124 그리고 배에 타고 있는 모든 사람들에게는 다른 사람들에게 해 줄 다정한 말이 있었다. 모든 사람이 파티와 의식에 함께했다. 모두들 먼 곳에 있는, 자신들이 소중하게 생각하는 사람들을 떠올렸다. 모두가 그들도 자신들을 떠올리게 되어 행복해 한다는 것을 알았다.

그것은 스크루지에게는 커다란 놀라움이었고, 스크루지는 바람 소리에 귀를 기울였다. 스크루지는 어두운, 미지의 바다를 항해하는 것이 얼마나 외로울지 생각해 보고 있었다. 바다는 죽음만큼이나 오래된 비밀을 간직하고 있었다. 생각에 잠겨 있을 때 웃음소리를 듣는 것은 스크루지에게 커다란 놀라움이었다. 그것이 자기 조카의 웃음소리라는 것을 알아차린 것은 스크루지에게 훨씬 더 큰 놀라움이었다. 스크루지는 이제 밝고 뽀송뽀송하고 빛나는 방 안에 있었다. 유령은 스크루지의 옆에서 미소를 짓고 서서 스크루지의 바로 그 조카를 즐겁게 바라보고 있었다!

"하하!" 스크루지의 조카가 웃었다. p.125 "하하하!"

웃음과 농담만큼 좋은 것도 아무것도 없다고 말하는 것이 당연하다. 자기 옆구리를 붙잡고 머리를 흔들고 얼굴 표정을 바꿔 가며 스크루지의 조카가 웃었을 때, 스크루지의 조카며느리 또한 웃었다. 그들의 친구들 또한 모두 웃었다. "하하! 하하하하!"

"삼촌은 크리스마스가 쓸데없는 것이라고 말씀하셨어!" 스크루지의 조카가 외쳤다. "삼촌은 또한 그렇게 믿고 계셨어!"

"그분한테는 참 안된 일이네요, 프레드!" 스크루지의 조카며느리가 말했다. 저런 여자들에게 축복이 있기를! 저런 여자들은 언제나 자기가 생각하는 것을 말한다. 그들은 언제나 솔직하다.

조카며느리는 아주 예뻤다. 그녀는 놀라운 외모의 눈부신 얼굴과 입 맞추고 싶게 만드는 듯한 작은 입을 가지고 있었다. 그녀는 초롱초롱 빛나는 눈을 가지고 있었다! 그녀는 무척 아름다웠지만, 또한 말 붙이기가 아주 편안하고 쉬웠다.

p.126 "삼촌은 재미있는 노인네이셔." 스크루지의 조카가 말했다. "그것은 사실이지. 삼촌이 더 즐거우실 수도 있을 텐데. 하지만 그분은 스스로를 벌주고 계시는 것뿐이고 나는 삼촌의 뜻에 거스르면서 할 말이 아무것도 없어."

"그분이 아주 부자라는 것은 확실하죠, 프레드." 스크루지의 조카며느리가 말했다. "적어도 당신이 늘 그렇게 말하니까요."

"그러면 뭐 해, 여보?" 스크루지의 조카가 말했다. "삼촌의 돈은 삼촌에게 아무 소용도 없어. 그 돈은 아무 도움이 안 되잖아. 삼촌은 그 돈으로 편하게 지내시지도 못하셔. 그 돈을 나눠 쓸 사람이 아무도 없으시지."

"나는 그런 분에 대해서는 참을성이 없어요." 스크루지의 조카며느리가 말했다. 스크루지의 조카며느리의 여자형제들과 다른 모든 여자들이 같은 의견을 가지고 있었다.

"오, 나는 있어!" 스크루지의 조카가 말했다. "나는 삼촌이 안쓰러워. 아무리 노력해도 삼촌께는 화낼 수가 없어. p.127 삼촌은 고통 받는 분이셔. 삼촌은 우리를 싫어하기로 작정하시고, 우리와 함께 저녁 식사를 하지 않으시지. 그것이 우리 마음을 아프게 하지는 않잖아. 삼촌은 저녁 식사를 놓친 분이신 거야."

"정말로 그분은 아주 훌륭한 저녁 식사를 놓치셨다고 생각해요." 스크루지의 조카며느리가 말했다. 다른 사람들도 모두 같은 말을 했다. 그들은 방금 저녁 식사를 마쳤고 식탁 위에는 후식이 있었다. 그들은 등불 옆 난롯가 주위에 모여 있었다.

"음, 그 말을 들으니 기쁘군." 스크루지의 조카가 말했다. "나는 이 젊은 가정부들에 대해 큰 믿음이 없었거든. 자네는 무슨 말을 할 텐가, 토퍼?"

토퍼는 분명히 스크루지의 조카며느리의 자매들 중 한 명에게 관심이 있었는데, 그가 총각은 그런 문제는 잘 모른다고 건성으로 대답했기 때문이었다. 스크루지의 조카며느리의 여동생은 얼굴을 붉혔다.

p.128 "계속해 봐요, 프레드." 스크루지의 조카며느리가 손뼉을 치며 말했다. "프레드는 말하기 시작하는 것을 끝내는 법이 없어요. 정말 엉뚱한 사람이라니까!"

웃지 않을 수가 없었기 때문에 스크루지의 조카는 다시 웃었다. 조카며느리의 여동생은 웃지 않으려고 했지만, 그녀 역시 웃기 시작했다.

"나는 단지 삼촌이 우리를 싫어하시고 우리와 함께 즐거워지기를 싫어하시기 때문에 어떤 즐거운 순간들을 잃어버리신다고 말하려던 것뿐이야. 삼촌이 당신의 낡은 사무실이나 먼지투성이 방들에서 발견할 수 있는 것들보다는 우리가 더 유쾌한 친구들이라는 것을 나는 확신해. 삼촌이 좋아하시든 좋아하지 않으시든 나는 매년 삼촌께 같은 기회를 드리려는 거야.

삼촌이 가엾으니까. 삼촌은 돌아가실 때까지 크리스마스를 증오하실지도 모르지만, 만약 내가 매년 기분 좋게 그곳에 가면 분명히 조금은 크리스마스를 좋아하실 거야. 누가 알아? 어쩌면 삼촌은 기분이 좋아지시고 그분의 서기에게 크리스마스 선물을 주실지도 몰라. 나는 내가 어제 삼촌의 마음을 바꾸어 놓았을지도 모른다고 생각해."

p.129 스크루지의 마음을 바꾸었다는 생각에 그들은 모두 웃었다. 스크루지의 조카는 성격이 좋았으므로 그들이 비웃는 것을 신경 쓰지 않았다. 조카는 그들이 계속 웃도록 부추겼다. 조카는 그들에게 술병을 건넸다.

차를 마신 후, 그들은 노래를 몇 곡 불렀다. 그들은 음악적인 가족이었고 자기들이 무엇을 잘하는지 알고 있었다. 토퍼는 아주 저음으로 노래를 부를 수 있었고 어떠한 압박감도 느끼지 않았다. 스크루지의 조카며느리는 하프를 잘 연주했다. 그녀는 스크루지의 여동생이 부르곤 했던 아주 간단한 노래를 연주했다.

이 곡이 시작되었을 때, 유령이 스크루지에게 보여 준 모든 것들이 스크루지의 마음속에 떠올랐다. 스크루지의 마음은 점점 더 누그러졌다. 만약 자신이 몇 년 전에 그 노래를 좀 더 자주 들었더라면 자신이 보다 친절해지고 행복해졌을지도 모른다고 스크루지는 생각했다.

p.130 하지만 그들이 저녁 내내 노래를 부른 것은 아니었다. 잠시 후, 그들은 카드놀이를 했는데, 때로는 아이들이 되는 것이 좋기 때문이며, 그러기에 크리스마스보다 더 좋은 때가 없기 때문이다. 우선 까막잡기를 했다. 토퍼는 정말로 눈을 감은 것이 아니었다. 스크루지의 조카는 토퍼에게 자기 아내의 여동생을 뒤쫓을 기회를 주려고 이 게임을 선택했다. 토퍼는 어색하게 그 여동생을 어디든 따라다녔다. 토퍼는 그 밖의 다른 사람은 잡으려고 하지 않았다.

그녀는 그것이 공정하지 않다고 종종 소리쳤고, 실제로도 그렇지 않았다. 하지만 그녀는 그로부터 계속 달아나려고 했음에도 불구하고 마침내 토퍼가 그녀를 잡았을 때, 그는 그녀를 구석으로 몰았고, 그녀는 도망칠 수가 없었다.

토퍼는 자신은 그녀가 누구인지 모르는 것처럼 행동했다. 눈을 감고서 토퍼는 그녀의 얼굴과 몸을 계속해서 더듬었다. 마침내 토퍼는 그녀의 손가락에 반지를 끼우고 목에 목걸이를 걸어 주었을 때 멈추었다! 그들이 함께 커튼 뒤에 숨었을 때, 그녀가 토퍼에게 그 일에 관한 자신의 의견을 말했다는 것에는 의심의 여지가 없었다.

p.131 스크루지의 조카며느리는 까막잡기는 하지 않았지만 안락한 구석에 있는 커다란 의자에 앉아 휴대용 발판에 발을 뻗고 편안하게 있었다. 유령과 스크루지는 그녀의 뒤에 바짝 붙어 있었다. 하지만 그녀는 나중에 놀이에 합류했고, 자기 남편에 관해 수많은 칭찬을 했다.

또한 어떻게, 언제, 어디에서 게임을 해도 스크루지의 조카며느리는 아주 잘했다. 스크루지의 조카가 내심 기뻐할 정도로 조카며느리는 자기 자매들보다 훨씬 더 잘했다. 젊은이와 늙은이 할 것 없이 그곳에는 스무 명의 사람들이 있었던 듯한데, 그들은 모두 놀이를 했고, 스크루지도 그랬다.

스크루지는 놀이에 아주 흥미를 느껴서 자신의 목소리가 그들의 귀에 들리지 않는다는 것을 완전히 잊었다. p.132 스크루지는 때때로 자신이 추측한 것을 아주 큰 소리로 소리 지르기도 했고, 꽤 자주 아주 잘 추측하기도 했다. 스크루지는 실제로 아주 머리가 좋았다.

유령은 스크루지가 노는 것을 보게 되어 대단히 기뻤고 미소를 지으며 그를 바라보았다. 스크루지는 손님들이 떠날 때까지 자신을 머무르게 해 달라고 유령에게 어린아이처럼 졸랐다. 하지만 유령은 그렇게 할 수 없다고 말했다.

"이제 새로운 놀이네요." 스크루지가 말했다. "30분만이요, 유령님, 딱 한 번만 봐 주세요!"

그것은 스크루지의 조카가 생각해 낸 것이 틀림없는 무언가에 '네', '아니오'를 외치는 놀이로 나머지 사람들은 무엇인지 알아내야 했다. 조카는 그들의 질문에 '네' 혹은 '아니요'로만 대답했다. 조카가 들은 첫 번째 질문은 그가 동물, 살아 있는 동물, 화난 동물, 야생 동물을 생각하고 있다는 것을 드러내었다. 그것은 때때로 으르렁거리고 투덜거리는 동물이었다. 그것은 심지어 때때로 말도 했다! 그것은 런던에 살고 거리를 돌아다녔다.

p.133 하지만 그것은 공연 속에 있지 않았다! 아무도 그것과 함께 걷지 않았고, 그것은 동물원에 살지도 않았다. 그것은 시장에서 도살된 적도 없었고 말도, 당나귀도, 암소도, 황소도, 호랑이도, 개도, 돼지도, 고양이도, 혹은 곰도 아니었다. 자신이 받은 모든 새로운 질문에 스크루지의 조카는 새롭게 웃음보를 터뜨렸다. 스크루지의 조카는 하도 많이 웃어서 일어서서 땅에 발을 동동 굴러야 했다. 마침내 조카며느리의 여동생도 미친 듯이 웃기 시작했다.

"제가 답을 알아냈어요!" 조카며느리의 여동생이 외쳤다. "제가 그것이 무엇인지 알아요, 프레드 형부! 제가 그것이 무엇인지 알아요!"

"그것이 무엇인데?" 프레드가 외쳤다.

"형부의 삼촌이신 스크루지 영감님이잖아요!"

확실히 그랬다. 모두 이 대답에 기뻐했으며 역시 웃기 시작했다.

p.134 "삼촌은 우리에게 많은 오락거리를 제공해 오셨어." 스크루지의 조카가 말했다. "삼촌의 건강을 위해 술을 마시지 않는다면 배은망덕한 일일 거야. 다들 적포도주 잔을 들고 준비해! 그럼, '스크루지 삼촌에게 은총이 함께 하기를!'"

"스크루지 삼촌을 위하여 건배!" 그들이 외쳤다.

"삼촌이 어떤 분이시든 즐거운 크리스마스를 보내시고 새해 복 많이 받으시기를!" 스크루지의 조카가 말했다. "삼촌은 저한테 이런 인사를 받지 않으려고 하시겠지만, 아무튼 받으셨으면 좋겠어요, 스크루지 삼촌!"

스크루지는 갑자기 아주 행복해지고 감동을 받아서 유령이 그에게 시간을 주었더라면 자기 조카에게 감사했을 것이었다. 하지만 조카의 입에서 나온 마지막 말이 끝나기 무섭게 모든 장면이 바뀌었다. 스크루지와 유령은 다시 이동 중이었다.

그들은 많은 것을 보았고, 멀리 갔고, 많은 집을 방문했지만, 늘 행복한 결말을 맞았다. p.135 유령은 병상 옆에 서 있었고 환자들은 즐거워했다. 타지에서는 사람들이 자기 집에 있는 듯 편히 있었다. 고군분투하는 사람들조차도 더 큰 것들을 바라며 참을성을 가졌다.

가난한 사람들조차도 부자가 된 기분이었다. 노숙자 수용소, 병원, 감옥에, 그리고 사람들이 크리스마스에 대해 마음의 문을 닫지 않았던 모든 슬픈 장소에 유령은 들렀다. 유령은 그들 모두에게 축복을 내렸다. 그것이 단지 하룻밤이라면 그것은 아주 긴 밤이었다. 하지만 스크루지는 이에 대해 의구심을 가졌는데, 크리스마스 휴일이 모두 동시에 지나가는 것 같았기 때문이었다.

또한 스크루지는 똑같아 보이는 반면에 유령은 점점 늙어 가는, 분명히 더 늙어 가는 것도 이상했다. 스크루지는 이러한 변화를 보았지만, 그들이 아이들의 파티를 떠날 때까지 그것에 대해 언급하지 않았다. p.136 그런 다음 스크루지는 그들이 공터에 함께 서 있는 동안 유령을 보았을 때, 유령의 머리카락이 백발인 것을 보았다.

"유령들의 삶은 그렇게 짧은가요?" 스크루지가 물었다.

"이승에서의 나의 삶은 아주 짧아." 유령이 대답했다. "오늘 밤에 끝나지."

"오늘 밤이라고요!" 스크루지가 외쳤다.

"오늘 밤 자정에!" 유령이 말했다. "귀를 기울여 봐! 그 시간이 오고 있어."

그 순간 시계가 11시 45분을 알리고 있었다.

"내가 이런 것을 물어 봐도 되는지 모르겠네요." 유령의 옷을 자세히 바라보며 스크루지가 말했다. "그런데 유령님의 몸의 한 부분은 아닌데, 이상한 무엇인가가 유령님의 옷 밑에서 보이네요. 발인가요, 아니면 갈고리 발톱인가요?"

"갈고리 발톱일지도 몰라. 왜냐하면 표면에 껍질이 있으니까." 유령이 구슬프게 대답했다. "여기를 봐."

p.137 유령의 옷 안에서 두 명의 아이가 나왔다. 그들은 가난하고 더럽고 아프고 슬퍼 보였다. 그들은 유령의 발치에 꿇어앉았고 유령의 옷 바깥쪽을 움켜잡았다.

"오, 이런!" 유령이 외쳤다. "여기를 봐. 봐 봐, 보라고, 이 아래를!"

그들은 소년과 소녀였다. 누렇고 마르고 못생기고 험상궂고 늑대 같았다. 하지만 그들은 구걸하면서 조용히 고개를 숙이고 있었다. 나이로 보면, 그들은 어리고 즐겁고 명랑해 보였어야 했지만, 무엇인가가 그들을 아주 늙고 지치게 보이도록 만들었다. 그들은 천사처럼 보였어야 했으나, 그 대신에 그들은 악마처럼 보였다. 이 아이들처럼 사람들을 깜짝 놀라게 하는 괴물이나 악마는 없었다.

스크루지는 혐오감을 느끼며 뒤로 물러났다. 스크루지는 아이들에 관해 말해 줄 무엇인가 좋은 말을 생각해 보려고 애썼다. p.138 스크루지는 무엇인가 나쁜 말을 하고 싶지는 않았지만, 거짓말을 할 수는 없었다. 말이 스크루지의 입 밖으로 나오려고 하지 않았다.

"유령님!" 스크루지가 말했다. "당신의 아이들인가요?"

"인간의 아이들이다." 그들을 내려다보며 유령이 말했다. "그리고 그들은 나에게 자기 아버지를 도와 달라고 조르며 나를 꽉 껴안고 있지. 이 소년은 '무지'야. 이 소녀는 '빈곤'이고. 너는 그들 둘 다를 경계해야 해. 하지만 무엇보다도 이 소년을 경계하도록. 이 아이의 얼굴에서 나는 '파멸'을 봐. 세상의 종말을 보는 것이지. 그것을 변화시키도록 해!"

"아이들한테는 집이나 음식이 없나요?" 스크루지가 물었다.

"감옥이 없냐고?" 유령은 스크루지가 과거에 했던 말을 되풀이하여 말했다. "구빈원은 없냐고?"

종이 12시를 쳤다.

스크루지는 유령을 찾아 주위를 둘러보았지만, 유령은 보이지 않았다. 마지막 종이 울리기를 멈추자 스크루지는 제이콥 말리가 자신에게 한 말이 기억났다. p.139 스크루지는 위를 올려다보았다. 스크루지는 긴 로브를 입고 두건을 쓰고 있는 심각한 표정의 과묵한 유령이 안개 속에서 나와 자신에게 다가오는 것을 보았다.

세 유령들 중 마지막 유령

p.140 유령은 천천히, 조용히 다가갔다. 유령이 자기 근처에 다가왔을 때, 스크루지는 무릎을 꿇고 앉았다. 유령은 짙은 검은색 옷을 입고 있었고, 그 옷은 유령의 머리, 얼굴, 그리고 몸을 가리고 있었다. 스크루지가 볼 수 있는 유령의 몸의 유일한 부분은 한쪽 손이었다. 만약 손을 보지 않았더라면, 스크루지는 어두운 밤에 그 유령을 볼 수 없었을 터였다.

p.141 유령이 자기 옆에 왔을 때, 스크루지는 유령이 키가 크고 고귀하며, 그 신비한 존재가 자신의 마음을 공포로 채웠다고 느꼈다. 스크루지는 더 이상은 알지 못했는데, 유령이 말을 하지도, 움직이지도 않았기 때문이었다.

"제가 미래의 크리스마스 유령 앞에 있는 것인가요?" 스크루지가 물었다.

유령은 대답하지 않았지만 손으로 무언가를 가리켰다.

"유령님은 일어나지 않았지만 장차 일어날 일들의 환영을 제게 막 보여 주려고 하시는군요?" 스크루지가 물었다. "그렇습니까, 유령님?"

유령의 옷의 두건이 마치 유령이 고개를 돌린 것처럼 약간 움직였다. 그것이 스크루지가 받은 유일한 대답이었다. 비록 이제는 유령들에게 익숙해졌지만, 스크루지는 그 침묵하는 형상이 아주 많이 두려워서 그의 다리 아래쪽은 후들거렸다. p.142 스크루지는 유령을 따라가려고 애쓸 때 거의 서 있을 수도 없을 지경이라는 것을 깨달았다. 유령은 스크루지를 바라보며 잠깐 멈추어 서서 기다렸다.

하지만 이것은 스크루지의 기분을 더 악화시켰다. 스크루지는 공포에 사로잡혔다. 스크루지는 두건 뒤에 자신을 주의 깊게 지켜보는 유령의 눈이 있다는 것을 생각하고 싶지 않았다. 그동안 스크루지는 오직 한쪽 손만 볼 수 있었다.

"미래의 유령님!" 스크루지가 소리쳤다. "저는 제가 본 어느 유령님보다 당신이 더 무섭습니다. 하지만 유령님이 저를 도와서 저를 더 좋은 사람으로 바꾸어 주고 싶어 하신다는 것을 알기 때문에 유령님께 감사드릴 것입니다. 저에게 말씀을 하지 않으실 건가요?"

유령은 스크루지에게 대답하지 않았다. 손은 그들 앞을 똑바로 가리키고 있었다.

"계속 안내해 주세요!" 스크루지가 말했다. "계속 안내해 주세요! 밤은 빨리 지나갈 것이고, 제가 알기로는 저에게 귀중한 시간이니까요. 계속 안내해 주세요, 유령님!"

유령은 조용히 걸어가기 시작했다. **p.143** 스크루지는 유령의 옷의 그림자 안에 들어가 따라갔는데, 그 그림자가 그를 데려가는 것 같았다.

그들은 갑자기 어느 도시로 들어갔다. 그것은 놀라웠다! 그 도시는 미지의 장소에서 온 것 같았다! 하지만 그들은 그 도시의 한복판에 있었다. 사람들이 주머니 안에 동전을 짤랑거리며 분주히 이리저리 뛰어다녔고 무리지어 이야기하고 자신의 손목시계를 쳐다보았다. 그들은 스크루지가 종종 보았던 부류의 사람들이었다.

스크루지는 사업가들로 이루어진 작은 무리 옆에서 걸음을 멈추었다. 유령의 손이 그들을 가리키는 것을 보고 스크루지는 그들의 대화를 듣기 위해 다가갔다.

"아니, 아무튼 그것에 대해서는 나도 많이 알지는 못해." 엄청난 주걱턱인 거구의 뚱뚱한 남자가 말했다. "그가 죽었다는 것만 알 뿐이야."

"언제 죽었어?" 다른 사람이 물었다.

"어젯밤에 죽은 것 같아." 뚱뚱한 남자가 말했다.

p.144 "저런, 무슨 일이 있었던 거야?" 담배를 피우고 있던 세 번째 남자가 물었다. "그 사람은 절대 죽지 않을 거라고 생각했는데."

"아무도 모르는 일이지." 뚱뚱한 사람이 하품을 하며 말했다.

"자기 돈은 다 어떻게 했대?" 말할 때면 흔들리는 커다란 뾰루지가 코에 난 붉은 얼굴의 신사가 물었다.

"나는 못 들었어." 뚱뚱한 남자가 다시 하품을 하며 말했다. "아마도 자기 회사에 돈을 남겼겠지. 나에게는 돈을 안 남겼으니까. 그게 내가 아는 전부야."

이 농담에 모든 사람들이 웃었다.

"아주 조촐한 장례식이 될 것 같군." 뚱뚱한 남자가 말했다. "그 장례식에 가겠다는 사람이 누가 있을지도 모르겠어, 우리가 조문단을 만들어 자원하는 것은 어떨까?"

"만일 우리가 점심 식사를 제공받는다면 나는 가도 상관없어." 코에 뾰루지가 난 신사가 말했다. "하지만 나는 꼭 배를 채워야 해."

p.145 다시 웃음소리가 있었다.

"저기, 나는 갈 이유가 없어." 뚱뚱한 남자가 말했다. "나는 검은 장갑을 절대 끼지 않고, 점심도 절대 안 먹어. 하지만 만일 다른 사람들이 간다면 나도 가겠어. 생각해 보면, 내가 그의 가장 친한 친구였을지도 몰라. 우리는 조금 대화를 나누어 보기는 했거든. 잘 가게!"

말하던 사람과 듣던 사람들은 떠났고 다른 무리들과 섞였다. 스크루지는 그 사람들을 알았고 설명을 바라며 유령 쪽을 바라보았다. 유령은 거리로 떠돌아다녔다. 유령의 손가락은 만나고 있는 두 사람을 가리켰다. 스크루지는 설명이 이곳에 있을지도 모른다고 생각하며 다시 귀를 기울였다.

스크루지는 이 사람들도 아주 잘 알았다. 그들은 아주 부유하고, 대단히 중요한 사업가들이었다. 스크루지는 언제나 그들이 자신을 좋아하게 만들려고 애썼는데, 그것이 사업에 유리하기 때문이었다.

p.146 "안녕하세요?" 한 사람이 말했다.

"잘 지내시죠?" 다른 사람이 대답했다.

"저기!" 첫 번째 사람이 말했다. "마침내 악마 같은 영감이 죽었다죠, 네?"

"저도 그렇게 들었어요." 두 번째 남자가 말했다. "춥네요, 안 그러세요?"

"크리스마스 치고는 보통이죠." 첫 번째 사람이 말했다. "스케이트를 타지 않으시는가 보군요?"

"네, 네." 두 번째 남자가 말했다. "스케이트는 타지 않아요. 안녕히 가세요!"

다른 말은 없었다. 그것이 그들의 만남이었고, 그들의 대화였고, 그들의 작별이었다.

스크루지는 처음에 유령이 그처럼 하찮은 대화를 자신에게 듣게 하려는 것에 놀랐다. 하지만 스크루지는 또한 유령이 자신에게 보여 주는 것에는 무엇인가 숨겨진 이유가 있는 것이 분명하다고 생각했다. 스크루지는 그 이유가 무엇일지에 관해 생각했다. 그들은 제이콥에 대해서는 말하고 있을 수 없었는데, 이곳은 미래였기 때문이었다.

p.147 스크루지는 사람들이 이야기할지도 모르는, 자신이 아는 누군가를 생각해 낼 수도 없었다. 하지만 그들이 이야기하고 있는 누구든 자신에게 가르쳐 줄 무엇인가를 가지고 있다는 것은 의심하지 않았다. 그래서 스크루지는 모든 이야기를 자세히 듣기로 결정했다.

스크루지는 자신의 환영을 찾아 주위를 둘러보았지만, 다른 사람이 자기가 평소에 있던 구석에 서 있었다. 비록 시계는 자신이 그곳에 있는 하루 중 평소와 같은 시각을 가리켰지만, 스크루지는 자기 모습을 보지 못했다. 하지만 그것이 스크루지를 그다지 놀래지는 않았다. 스크루지는 자신의 삶을 바꾸기로 결정하고 있었던 터였으며, 자신이 이제는 그러한 변화 후에 어떤 일이 일어났는지 보고 있는 것이라고 생각하고 또 그러기를 바랐다.

유령은 손으로 가리키며 조용히 어둠 속에서 스크루지 옆에 서 있었다. 이런저런 생각을 하는 것을 멈추었을 때 스크루지는 다시 유령을 바라보았다. 스크루지는 다시 자신에게 고정된 유령의 눈을 상상했다. p.148 그것은 스크루지의 몸을 떨리게 했고 오싹한 기분이 느껴지게 했다.

그들은 분주한 장면을 떠나 스크루지가 전에 한 번도 가 본 적이 없는, 시내의 조금 알려진 곳으로 갔다. 그곳이 시내에서 잘 사는 쪽이 아니라는 것을 스크루지는 알아차렸다. 길은 위험하고 좁았다. 상점과 집들은 가난해 보였고, 사람들은 반은 헐벗고 취해 있고 추했다. 골목길은 오물로 가득 차 있었다. 그곳은 범죄와 고통의 냄새가 났다.

그들은 마침내 쇠붙이, 누더기, 병, 뼈다귀, 유지를 파는 가게에 도착했다. 안쪽의 바닥에는 녹슨 열쇠, 못, 쇠사슬, 경첩, 줄, 저울, 저울추, 그리고 온갖 쇠붙이들이 있었다. 알려지지 않는 것이 더 나은 비밀들이 뼈다귀, 쇠붙이, 그리고 유지 아래에 숨겨져 있었다.

오래된 벽돌로 만들어진 난로 옆, 가게 안에 있는 상품들 사이에는 거의 일흔 살은 된 백발의 남자가 앉아 있었다. p.149 날씨가 추웠는데도 불구하고 그는 누더기만 걸치고 있었다. 그는 파이프 담배를 피웠고 느긋했다.

스크루지와 유령은 무거운 꾸러미를 든 여자가 상점 안으로 들어오는 순간 막 이 남자를 보았다. 하지만 그녀가 막 들어왔을 때, 역시 꾸러미를 들고 있는 다른 여자도 안으로 들어왔다. 그녀 뒤로 빛깔이 바랜 검은 옷을 입은 한 남자가 바짝 따라왔다. 서로를 알아보았을 때, 그들은 모두 놀란 것 같았다. 잠시 놀란 후, 세 사람은 모두 웃음을 터뜨렸다.

"청소부 여자가 가장 먼저가 되게 해 주세요." 가장 먼저 들어온 여자가 소리쳤다. "세탁부를 두 번째, 장의사 남자를 세 번째로 해 주시고요. 여기를 보세요, 조 영감님! 우리가 모두 서로를 만났군요!"

"이보다 더 나은 곳에서는 만날 수도 없지." 입에서 파이프 담배를 떼며 조 영감이 말했다. p.150 "거실로 오게. 자네들이 낯선 사람들도 아니잖나. 내가 가게를 닫지. 아! 내 몸의 뼈와 이 문들은 둘 다 움직일 때 엄청 시끄럽군! 하하! 우리 모두 잘 어울리는군. 거실로 들어오게. 거실로 들어와."

거실은 넝마 조각들 뒤에 있는 작은 공간이었다. 노인은 불을 피우고 자신의 파이프 담배로 등불을 켰다. 노인은 입에 파이프를 다시 물고 담배를 다시 피우기 시작했다.

조 영감이 이 일을 하는 동안, 이미 말문을 연 여자는 자기 꾸러미를 바닥에 던지고 의자에 앉았다. 그녀는 무릎 위에 팔꿈치를 교차시켜 올려놓았다. 그녀는 다른 두 사람을 거만하게 바라보았다.

"모든 사람이 자기 몸은 스스로 돌봐야 해, 딜버." 청소부 여자가 말했다. "그 사람도 늘 그랬잖아."

"맞아, 정말 그랬지!" 세탁부가 말했다.

"그렇다면 겁먹은 것처럼 나를 빤히 쳐다보지 마." 청소부 여자가 말했다. p.151 "우리가 서로에 대해 경찰에 말하려는 것은 아닌 거지?"

"아니야, 정말로!" 딜버 부인과 남자가 같이 말했다. "우리가 그런 일을 바라서는 안 되지."

"그렇다면 아주 잘 됐군!" 청소부 여자가 외쳤다. "충분해. 그가 죽었고 이 물건들을 더 이상 필요로 하지 않는다는 것에 우리 모두 동의해."

"그래." 딜버 부인이 웃으며 말했다.

"만약 그가 자신이 죽은 후에도 그것들을 가지고 있기를 바랐다면, 생전에 왜 좀 더 친절하지 않았냐는 말이지?" 청소부 여자가 말했다. "만약 그랬다면, 죽어갈 때 혼자 죽는 대신에 자기를 돌봐줄 사람이 누군가는 있었을 텐데."

"지금까지 들은 말 중 가장 옳은 말이야." 딜버 부인이 말했다.

"그에게 무언가 더 안 좋은 일이 일어나면 좋겠어." 여자가 말했다. p.152 "무언가 더 안 좋은 일이 일어날 거야. 내가 그의 집에서 가져온 물건 꾸러미를 열어 봐요, 조 영감님. 그리고 그것이 얼마나 나가는지 말해 줘요. 솔직히요. 내가 먼저가 되어도 두렵지 않고, 저 사람들이 제 꾸러미를 보아도 두렵지 않아요. 내가 알기로는 우리가 그의 집에서 물건을 가지고 온 것을 우리 모두 아니까요. 그 일이 나쁘지는 않네요. 꾸러미를 열어 봐요, 조 영감님."

하지만 그녀의 친구들은 그녀가 먼저가 되는 것을 원하지 않았다. 빛바랜 검은 옷을 입은 남자가 먼저 자기 꾸러미를 열었다. 그것은 그리 많지는 않았다. 도장 한두 개, 필통 한 개, 소매 단추 한 쌍, 그리고 브로치 한 개였다. 아무것도 비싸 보이지 않았다. 그것들은 조 영감에 의해 몇 차례 조사되고 값이 매겨졌다. 조 영감은 분필로 벽에 가격을 썼고 그것들을 모두 더했다.

"그게 총액이야." 조 영감이 말했다. "이보다 한 푼도 더 줄 수는 없어. 다음은 누구지?"

딜버 부인이 다음이었다. 그녀는 침대보와 수건들, 옷가지 몇 벌, 두 개의 오래된 은 찻숟가락, 그리고 장화 몇 켤레를 가지고 있었다. p.153 그녀의 총액은 같은 방식으로 벽에 제시되었다.

"나는 언제나 여자들한테는 너무 많이 준다니까." 조 영감이 말했다. "그것이 나의 약점이고, 내가 스스로를 망치는 길이지. 그것이 총액이라네. 만약 나에게 한 푼이라도 더 달라고 부탁을 해도 나는 그것을 주지 않을 거야."

"그리고 이제 내 꾸러미를 풀어 보세요, 조 영감님." 첫 번째 여자가 말했다.

조 영감은 꾸러미를 푸는 것을 더 쉽게 하려고 무릎을 꿇고 앉았다. 조 영감은 어떤 거무스름한 물건이 돌돌 말린 무거운 물건을 꺼냈다.

"이것은 뭐라고 부르는 물건이지?" 조 영감이 말했다. "침대 커튼이잖아!"

"아!" 웃으면서 팔짱을 낀 채 몸을 앞으로 굽히며 청소부 여자가 말했다. "침대 커튼이죠!"

"그가 그곳에 죽어서 누워 있는데, 그 커튼을 내렸다고 말하려는 것은 아니겠지?" 조 영감이 물었다.

p.154 "아니요, 맞아요." 청소부 여자가 대답했다. "안 되나요?"

"자네는 큰돈을 벌려고 태어났구먼." 조 영감이 말했다. "자네는 반드시 그럴 거야."

"나는 확실히 그와 같은 사람한테서 물건을 가져오는 것이 나쁘게 느

꺼지지 않아요." 청소부 여자가 냉담하게 말했다. "저기, 그 담요에 기름을 떨어뜨리지 말아요."

"그 사람의 담요인가?" 조 영감이 물었다.

"달리 누구의 것이라고 생각하세요?" 청소부 여자가 말했다. "그 사람은 죽었어요. 그 사람이 춥다고 누가 상관이나 하겠어요?"

"그가 당신이 걸릴 수도 있는 어떤 병으로 죽은 것은 아니기를 바라네, 응?" 조 영감이 자기 일을 멈추고 위를 쳐다보며 말했다.

"그런 점은 걱정하지 마세요." 청소부 여자가 말했다. "나도 무언가를 옮을 만큼 그 사람의 시체 주변에 오래 머무를 정도로 그 사람을 좋아하는 것은 아니라고요. 아! 저 셔츠를 눈이 아플 때까지 오래 살펴보셔도 되지만, 구멍 하나 없다고요. p.155 그것은 그가 가지고 있는 것 중에 가장 좋은 것이고 비싼 것이기도 해요. 내가 없었다면 그 옷을 낭비하는 꼴이었을 거예요."

"그것이 낭비되었을 거란 말이 무슨 뜻인가?" 조 영감이 물었다.

"그가 그 셔츠를 입은 채 매장되었을 것이라는 뜻이죠." 여자가 웃으며 대답했다. "누군가가 멍청하게도 그렇게 해 놓았지만, 내가 다시 벗겨냈답니다. 그 옷은 근사해 보이지만, 아무것도 그를 잘생겨 보이게 만들지는 못할 거예요."

스크루지는 공포에 사로잡힌 채 이 말을 들었다. 그들은 자기들이 훔친 물건들 주변에 모여 앉았다. 영감의 등불로 제공된 흐릿한 불빛 속에서 스크루지는 그들을 역겨워하며 지켜보았다. 스크루지는 죽은 사람의 물건들을 팔고 있었기 때문에 그들이 악마 같다고 생각했다.

"하하!" 조 영감이 그들에게 돈을 주었을 때 세탁부 여자가 웃었다. "보시다시피, 이것이 일의 결말이로군요. p.156 그는 살아 있을 때 모두를 위협하여 쫓아냈어요! 하지만 그가 죽으니까 우리가 그의 물건을 가질 수 있네요!"

"유령님!" 스크루지가 머리에서 발끝까지 덜덜 떨며 말했다. "알겠어요, 알겠어. 이 불행한 남자의 경우가 제 경우가 될지도 모른다는 거잖아요. 제 삶이 이렇게 되어 가고 있어요. 맙소사, 이것이 무엇인가요?"

스크루지는 공포에 사로잡혀 뒤로 껑충 뛰어 물러났는데 장면이 바뀌었기 때문이었다. 지금 스크루지는 침대, 커튼이 없는 맨 침대에 거의 닿을 뻔했다. 침대보 밑에는 무엇인가가 덮여 있었다. 방은 아주 어두웠다. 너무나 어두워서 확실히 보이지는 않았다.

그러나 스크루지는 아무튼 주변을 둘러보았고, 그것이 어떤 종류의 방인지 알고 싶어 했다. 바깥 공기에서 피어 나오는 옅은 불빛이 침대 위로 곧장 떨어졌다. 모든 것이 도난당하고 아무도 지켜보지 않으며 아무도 상관하지 않는 이 침대 위에는 이 남자의 시신이 있었다.

스크루지는 유령을 쳐다보았다. 유령의 확고부동한 손은 시신의 머리를 가리킨 채였다. p.157 만약 스크루지가 그 시신의 머리를 덮어 놓은 덮개를 조금 옮겼다면, 그 남자의 얼굴을 볼 수 있었을 것이었다. 스크루지는 그런 생각이 들었고, 그렇게 하는 것이 얼마나 쉬울지 느꼈고, 그렇게 하기를 열망했다. 하지만 스크루지는 어느 것도 움직일 힘이 없었다.

오, 냉혹하고 끔찍한 죽음이여, 여기서는 네가 왕이다! 만일 누군가가 사랑 받거나 존경받는다면, 죽음은 그를 나쁘게 혹은 두려워 보이게 만들지 않는다. 만약 그가 용감하고 고상하고 진실하다면, 그의 죽음은 다를 것이다! 사람들은 그의 죽음에 대해 다르게 생각할 것이다!

어떠한 목소리도 이 남자를 위해 울어 주지 않았으나, 스크루지는 이 남자를 위해 울어 주고 싶었다. 만일 이 남자가 다시 살아날 수 있다면, 그가 무슨 생각을 할까 하고 스크루지는 생각했다. 그가 탐욕과 사업에 대해 생각할까? 그것들은 이 남자를 돕지 못했다!

p.158 그는 어둡고 빈 집에 그를 기억할 남자도, 여자도, 혹은 아이도 한 명 없이 누워 있었다. 스크루지는 혼자서 죽어 있는 죽은 남자에 관해 해 줄 무언가 친절한 말을 생각하려고 애썼다. 고양이는 문을 할퀴고 있었고, 마루 밑에서 쥐들의 소리도 나고 있었다. 스크루지는 왜 그것들이 방 안으로 들어오려고 하는지에 관해서는 생각하고 싶지 않았다.

"유령님!" 스크루지가 말했다. "이곳은 무시무시한 곳입니다. 우리가 떠나면 이곳의 교훈을 잊지 않겠어요. 저를 믿어 주세요. 가요!"

그래도 유령은 확고부동한 손가락으로 시체의 머리를 가리켰다.

"유령님을 이해해요." 스크루지가 말했다. "할 수 있다면 저도 보겠어요. 하지만 저는 그럴 힘이 없어요, 유령님. 힘이 없다고요."

다시 유령은 스크루지를 바라보는 듯했다.

"만약 이 마을에서 이 남자의 죽음으로 인해 슬픔을 느끼는 어떤 사람이 있다면, 그 사람을 저에게 보여 주세요, 유령님." 스크루지가 몹시 고통스러워하며 말했다. p.159 "부탁합니다!"

유령은 그의 거무스름한 옷을 날개처럼 열었다. 팔짱을 꼈을 때, 유령은 어머니와 그녀의 아이들이 있는 햇빛이 비치는 방을 드러냈다.

그녀는 간절히 열망하며 누군가를 기다리고 있었다. 그녀는 방 안을 왔다 갔다 했다. 그녀는 모든 소리에 펄쩍 뛰었고 창문으로 밖을 내다보았다. 그녀는 시계를 응시했다. 그녀는 바느질을 하려고 애썼지만 집중할 수가 없었다. 그녀는 놀고 있는 아이들의 목소리에도 짜증이 났다.

마침내 오래 기다리던 문 두드리는 소리가 들렸다. 그녀는 문으로 서둘러 달려갔고 그녀의 남편, 그러니까 젊지만 얼굴은 지치고 슬퍼 보이는 남자를 만났다. 그 남편의 눈에서 스크루지는 그가 숨기려고 하는 기쁨의 광채를 볼 수 있다고 생각했다.

p.160 그는 난롯가에서 자신을 기다리고 있었던 저녁 식사를 하려고 앉았다. 마침내 여자가 어떤 소식이 있는지 남자에게 물었을 때, 그 남자는 당혹스러워 보였다.

"좋은 소식이에요?" 그녀가 물었다. "나쁜 소식이에요?"

"나쁜 소식이야." 그가 대답했다.

"우리가 완전히 파산한 것인가요?" 그녀가 물었다.

"아니." 그가 말했다. "아직 희망이 있어, 캐롤라인."

"만일 그 사람이 마음을 바꾸면 희망이 있죠!" 그녀가 말했다. "하지만 그것은 불가능해요."

"그 사람은 마음을 바꿀 수 없어." 남편이 말했다. "그 사람은 죽었으니까."

그녀는 차분하고 참을성 있는 사람이었지만, 이 소식을 듣고 마음속으로 감사했다. 그녀는 손뼉을 치면서 고맙다고 말했다. 그녀는 다음 순간 유감이라고 말했다. 하지만 그녀가 첫 번째로 느낀 것은 고맙다는 것이었다.

"그 술 취한 여자가 간밤에 나에게 말해 주었을 때 나는 믿지 않았어." 그가 말했다. "하지만 내가 오늘 확인해 봤지. 그것은 사실이었어. 그 사람은 그때 아플 뿐만 아니라 죽어 가고 있었던 거야."

p.161 "이제 우리는 누구에게 빚을 지고 있는 거죠?" 그녀가 물었다.

"나도 몰라." 그가 말했다. "하지만 그 전에 우리는 돈을 준비해 놓게 될 거야. 설령 우리가 그렇게 하지 못하더라도 새로운 사람은 그 사람보다는 더 친절할 거야. 우리, 오늘 밤에는 가벼운 마음으로 자도 돼, 캐롤라인."

그랬다. 그들의 마음은 한결 가벼웠다. 아이들의 얼굴은 더 밝아졌다! 이 남자가 죽었기 때문에 그 집안은 더 행복해졌다! 유령이 스크루지에게 보여줄 수 있었던 이 남자의 죽음으로 야기된 유일한 감정은 기쁨뿐이었다.

"이 죽음에 대해 누군가 슬퍼하는 것을 보여 주세요." 스크루지가 말했다. "아니면 우리가 방금 떠나온 그 어두운 방은 영원히 제 기억 속에 있게 될 거예요, 유령님."

유령은 스크루지를 그의 발에 익숙한 몇몇 거리로 데리고 갔다. p.162 그리고 그들이 걸어갈 때, 스크루지는 자신을 찾아보려고 여기저기를 보았으나, 아무 곳에도 자신은 없었다. 그들은 스크루지가 전에 방문한 적이 있는 집, 그러니까 가난한 밥 크래칫의 집으로 들어갔고, 어머니와 아이들이 불가에 앉아 있는 것을 보았다.

조용했다. 아주 조용했다. 시끄러운 크래칫가의 어린아이들은 한쪽 구석에서 움직이지 않고 있었다. 그들은 피터를 올려다보았는데, 피터는 자기 앞에 책을 두고 있었다. 어머니와 딸들은 바느질을 하느라고 바빴다. 하지만 분명히 그들은 조용했다!

"그리고 주님은 한 아이를 데려가 그를 그들 가운데 내려두셨노라." 피터가 말했다.

스크루지가 그 말을 어디에서 들었던가? 스크루지가 꿈속에서 그 말을 들은 적은 없었다. 스크루지와 유령이 집으로 들어올 때 그 소년이 그 구절을 큰 소리로 읽은 것이 분명했다. 왜 피터는 계속하지 않는 것일까?

어머니는 자신의 일감을 탁자 위에 놓았고 손을 얼굴로 들어 올렸다.

p.163 "색깔 때문에 눈이 아프구나." 그녀가 말했다.

색깔? 아, 막내 팀은 어디에 있지?

"이제 다시 괜찮구나." 크래칫의 아내가 말했다. "그 색깔은 촛불로 보기에는 좋지 않구나. 너희 아버지는 어디에 계시니? 너희 아버지가 집에 오실 시간이 거의 다 된 것이 분명한데."

"늦으시네요." 피터가 책을 덮으며 대답했다. "하지만 제 생각에는 요사이 지난 며칠 저녁 아버지가 이전보다 걸음이 더 느려지신 것 같아요, 어머니."

그들은 다시 아주 조용해졌다.

"너희 아버지가 막내 팀을 어깨에 태우고 아주 빨리 걷곤 하셨던 것이 기억나는구나." 그녀는 유쾌한 목소리를 내려고 애쓰면서 말했다.

"저도 그래요." 피터가 외쳤다. "자주요."

"저도요." 다른 아이가 소리쳤다. 모두가 소리쳤다.

"하지만 팀은 데리고 다니기에 아주 가벼웠어." 그녀가 자기 일에 집중하며 말했다. "그리고 아버지는 팀을 사랑하셔서 전혀 수고스러워하지 않으셨어. p.164 그런데 아빠가 문 앞에 계시는구나!"

그녀는 그를 맞으러 달려 나갔고, 담요를 두른 작은 체구의 밥이 안으로 들어왔다. 밥이 마실 차가 난로 위에 준비되어 있었고, 식구들은 모두 그 차를 그에게 주려고 했다. 그런 다음 두 명의 어린 크래칫 남매가 밥의 무릎 위에 앉아 그의 얼굴에 작은 뺨을 대었다.

밥은 아이들과 함께 있어 아주 명랑했고 가족 전부에게 기쁜 마음으로 말했다. 밥은 탁자 위에 있는 일감을 보고 디자인과 크래칫 부인과 딸들의 속도를 칭찬했다. 그들은 일요일이 되기 훨씬 전에 일을 끝낼 것이라고 밥은 말했다.

"일요일이요!" 밥의 아내가 말했다. "그럼 오늘도 가셨군요, 여보?"

"그래, 여보." 밥이 대답했다. "당신도 갈 수 있었다면 좋을 텐데. 그곳이 얼마나 푸른 곳인지 보았으면 당신에게도 좋았을 거야. 하지만 당신은 그곳을 자주 보게 될 거야. 일요일에 그곳으로 산책을 가겠다고 그 아이에게 약속했어. 어린 내 아들!" 밥이 외쳤다. p.165 "어린 내 아들!"

밥은 즉시 훌쩍이기 시작했다. 밥은 어쩔 수가 없었다. 밥은 방을 나가 위층에 있는 방에 들어갔는데, 그 방은 환하게 불이 켜져 있었고 크리스마스 장식물들이 매달려 있었다. 아이 옆에 가까이 앉는 의자가 있었고, 최근에 누군가가 그곳에 있었던 흔적이 있었다. 가엾은 밥은 그 의자에 앉았다. 우는 것을 그친 후, 밥은 다소 위안을 느꼈고 다시 아래층으로 내려갔다.

그들은 불가에 앉아 이야기를 나누었고, 여자아이들과 어머니는 여전히 일을 하고 있었다. 밥은 그들에게 스크루지의 조카의 놀라운 친절함에 대해 이야기해 주었는데, 밥은 스크루지의 조카를 한 번 만난 적이 있을 뿐이었다.

밥에 의하면, 그날 거리에서 자신을 만났을 때 자신이 다소 슬퍼 보이는 것을 보고, 스크루지의 조카가 자기에게 무슨 일이 일어나 낙담하고 있는지 물었다는 것이었다.

p.166 "그분은 이전에는 들어 본 적도 없는 가장 친절한 신사분이시라서 그분께 그 일에 대해 말씀드렸어." 밥이 말했다. "'그 일에 대해서는 진심으로 유감입니다, 크래칫 씨. 그리고 마음씨 고운 부인도 상심이 크시겠어요.'라고 그분이 말씀하시더군. 그런데 그분이 그것을 어떻게 아셨는지

나도 모르겠어."

"무엇을 알았다는 거예요, 여보?" 크래칫 부인이 물었다.

"아, 당신이 착한 아내라는 것 말이야." 밥이 대답했다.

"모두가 그것을 다 아는 걸요!" 피터가 말했다.

"맞았어, 얘야!" 밥이 외쳤다. "다른 사람들도 알면 좋겠구나. '마음씨 고운 부인이 정말 안 되셨습니다. 어떤 식으로든 제가 도울 수 있다면, 저를 찾아오세요.'라고 그분이 말씀하셨어. 그분은 아주 유쾌하셨어. 정말로 마치 그분이 우리 막내 팀을 알고 계셨고 우리와 함께 슬퍼하시는 듯했다고."

"그분은 착한 분이신 것이 확실하네요!" 크래칫 부인이 말했다.

"여보, 만약 당신이 그분을 보고 이야기를 나누어 보았다면 그 사실을 더욱 확신했을 거야." 밥이 말했다. p.167 "설령 그분이 피터에게 더 나은 일자리를 찾아주는 것을 도와주신다고 하더라도 나는 놀라지 않을 거야."

"아버지 이야기 들었니, 피터?" 크래칫 부인이 말했다.

"그러면 피터 오빠는 근사한 여자를 만날 거야." 딸들 가운데 한 명이 외쳤다. "그러면 오빠는 그 여자와 결혼할 수 있도록 돈을 저축하기 시작할 거야."

"오, 조용히 해!" 피터가 미소를 지으며 말했다.

"그런 일이 일어날 수 있지." 밥이 말했다. "장차 그럴 수 있어. 우리는 나중에 그런 생각을 할 수 있을 거야, 얘야. 하지만 우리가 어디를 가거나 무엇을 하더라도, 우리들 중 아무도 가엾은 막내 팀을 잊지 않을 거라고 나는 확신한단다. 그 아이는 우리들 중 이 세상을 떠난 첫 번째 아이니까."

"절대로 안 잊어요, 아버지!" 아이들이 외쳤다.

"그리고 나는 안다." 밥이 말했다. "얘들아, 비록 팀은 꼬마 아이였지만 팀이 얼마나 참을성 있고 얼마나 차분했는지 우리가 기억할 때면 우리끼리 말다툼을 하지 않게 될 거야."

p.168 "그럼요, 절대로요, 아버지." 그들 모두 다시 외쳤다.

"나는 아주 행복하구나." 밥이 말했다. "아주 행복해!"

크래칫 부인은 밥에게 입맞춤을 했고, 그의 딸들도 그에게 입맞춤을 했고, 두 명의 어린 크래칫 남매도 그에게 입맞춤을 했으며, 피터와 밥은 악수를 했다. 막내 팀, 너에게는 무언가 특별하고 아름다운 것이 있구나!

"유령님, 무언가가 유령님이 곧 떠나실 거라고 제게 말해 주는군요." 스크루지가 말했다. "저도 그것을 압니다만, 그 방법은 모르겠습니다. 죽은 사람이 누구인지 말씀해 주세요."

크리스마스의 유령은 스크루지를 다른 시간과 장소로 데리고 갔다. 유령은 많은 장소들을 통과하여 재빨리 이동했다. 유령은 어디에서도 스크루지가 쉬게 두거나 기다리게 하지 않았다.

"이 장소가 제가 미래에 살게 될 곳이라는 것을 알겠습니다." 스크루지가 말했다. "집이 보입니다. p.169 제가 미래에 어떻게 될지 보여 주세요!"

유령은 걸음을 멈추었고, 그의 손은 집을 가리키지 않았다.

"집은 저쪽에 있습니다." 스크루지가 소리쳤다. "왜 먼 곳을 가리키십니까?"

유령은 같은 것을 계속해서 가리켰다.

스크루지는 자기 사무실의 창문으로 달려가 안을 들여다보았다. 그것은 여전히 사무실이었지만 그의 것은 아니었다. 가구는 똑같지 않았고, 의자에 앉아 있는 사람도 스크루지가 아니었다. 유령은 여전히 반대쪽 방향을 가리켰다.

스크루지는 다시 유령을 따라갔고, 유령이 왜 이 길로 가고 있는 것인지 이상하게 생각하면서도 어느 철문에 도착할 때까지 유령을 따라갔다. 스크루지는 들어가기 전에 주위를 둘러보려고 걸음을 멈추었다. 그들은 교회의 경내에 있었다. p.170 이곳은 죽은 사람이 묻혀 있는 곳이었다. 이곳은 스크루지가 자기 이름을 알게 될 장소였다. 그것은 근사한 묘지가 아니었다. 벌초를 하거나 이곳에 아름다운 꽃을 심어 놓는 사람은 아무도 없었다.

유령은 무덤 가운데에 서 있었고, 한 무덤을 가리켰다. 스크루지는 벌벌 떨면서 그곳으로 다가갔다. 유령은 변함이 없었지만, 스크루지는 전보다 더 두려워했다.

"이 비석을 보기 전에, 저에게 무슨 말씀이라도 해 주세요." 스크루지가 말했다. "이것들은 일어날 상황의 환영인가요, 아니면 일어날 수도 있는 상황의 환영일 뿐인가요?"

여전히 유령은 자기가 서 있는 옆의 무덤 쪽, 그 아래쪽을 가리켰다.

"인간은 어떤 미래를 갖게 될지 몰라요." 스크루지가 말했다. "하지만 사람이 바뀌면 다른 미래를 가지겠지요, 그렇죠? 제가 이 비석을 보기 전에 이것이 사실이라고 제게 말씀해 주세요!"

유령은 여전히 움직이거나 말을 하지 않았다.

스크루지는 그곳을 향해 기어갔고, 가면서 덜덜 떨었다. 유령의 손가락을 따라가 스크루지는 방치된 무덤의 비석 위에서 자기 자신의 이름 에브니저 스크루지를 읽었다.

p.171 "침대에 누워 있던 남자가 저입니까?" 스크루지가 무릎을 꿇고 외쳤다.

유령의 손가락이 무덤을 가리켰다가 스크루지를 가리켰고, 다시 무덤을 가리켰다.

"안 돼요, 유령님!" 스크루지가 외쳤다. "오, 안 돼요, 안 돼!"

손가락은 여전히 그곳에 있었다.

"유령님!" 스크루지는 유령의 옷을 꽉 움켜잡고 외쳤다. "제 말 좀 들어 보세요! 저는 과거의 제가 아니에요. 저는 외롭게 죽는 사람이 되지 않을 거예요. 저에게 희망이 없다면, 왜 저에게 이런 것을 보여 주시나요?"

처음으로 유령의 손이 흔들리는 것 같았다.

"착한 유령님, 저는 유령님이 친절한 마음을 가지고 계신 것을 압니다." 스크루지가 말했다. "저를 동정하시는 것을 알아요. 제가 제 인생을 바꾸면 이러한 일들을 바꿀 수 있다고 제게 약속해 주세요!"

p.172 친절한 손이 덜덜 떨렸다.

"저는 마음속으로 크리스마스를 기리고 1년 내내 크리스마스 정신을 지키고자 애쓸 것입니다. 저는 과거, 현재, 미래의 유령님을 기억하며 살 것입니다. 세 분의 유령님들을 모두 제 마음속에 모시고 살 것입니다. 저는 유령님들이 저에게 가르쳐 주신 교훈에 귀를 기울일 것입니다. 오, 제가 이 비석의 비문을 지우게 될지 제게 말씀해 주세요."

고통을 느끼며 스크루지는 유령의 손을 움켜잡았다. 유령은 자기 손을 빼려고 애썼다. 마침내 유령이 더욱 강해졌기 때문에 유령은 스크루지에게서 자기 손을 빼냈다. 자신의 미래를 바꿔 달라고 하기 위한 마지막 기도로 손을 들어 올린 스크루지는 유령이 변하는 것을 보았다. 유령은 오그라들더니 침대 기둥으로 변했다.

일의 결말

p.173 그랬다! 그것은 자기 침대였다. 그중에서도 가장 좋고 가장 기쁜 것은 스크루지가 자기 인생을 바꿀 시간을 가졌다는 것이었다!

"저는 과거, 현재, 미래의 유령님을 기억하며 살겠습니다!" 스크루지가 침대에서 벌떡 일어나 나오며 다시 말했다. "세 유령님들을 제 마음속에 모시고 살 것입니다. **p.174** 오, 제이콥 말리! 하느님과 크리스마스가 이렇게 찬양받고 있네! 내가 이렇게 무릎을 꿇고 말하네, 제이콥, 이렇게 무릎을 꿇고 말일세!"

스크루지가 자신의 착한 생각에 너무나 기쁘고 너무나 열중는 바람에 그의 갈라진 목소리는 간신히 나올 지경이었다. 유령과 논쟁을 벌일 때 스크루지는 너무나 많이 울었던 터여서 그의 얼굴은 눈물로 젖어 있었다.

"도둑맞지 않았구나." 스크루지가 자신의 침대 커튼 중 하나를 품 안에 접으며 외쳤다. "아무도 내 침대 커튼을 훔치지 않았어. 그것들이 여기에 있다고. 내가 여기에 있어. 일어날지도 모르는 일들의 환영은 바뀔 수도 있는 거야. 그렇게 될 거야. 그렇게 될 것임을 나는 알아!"

스크루지의 손은 자신의 모든 옷을 만지고, 그것들을 돌려보고, 그것들을 입고, 그것들을 쥐어뜯고, 그것들을 가지고 춤을 추느라 분주했다.

"어떻게 해야 할지 모르겠어!" 스크루지가 웃고 울고 바보처럼 행동하며 외쳤다. "나는 깃털처럼 마음이 가벼워. 나는 천사처럼 행복해. **p.175** 나는 학생처럼 즐거워. 모든 사람들에게 즐거운 크리스마스가 되기를! 온 세상 사람들이 새해 복 많이 받기를! 어이, 안녕하시오! 어이! 안녕하시오!"

스크루지는 거실로 달려 나갔고 이제 숨을 헐떡이며 그곳에 서 있었다.

"내 수프가 있다!" 스크루지가 벽난로 주변을 뛰어다니며 말했다. "저기 제이콥 말리의 유령이 들어온 문이 있구나! 저기 현재의 크리스마스 유령이 앉아 있던 구석이 있어! 저기 떠돌아다니는 유령들을 본 창문이 있어. 모두 멀쩡하네. 모두 사실이었어. 모두 일어났다고. 하하하!"

정말로 수년 동안 웃지 않았던 사람치고 그것은 대단한 웃음이고 밝은 웃음이었다. 많은 새로운 웃음의 시작이었다!

"오늘이 며칠인지 모르겠구나!" 스크루지가 말했다. "내가 유령들과 얼마나 오래 지냈는지 모르겠어. **p.176** 아무것도 모르겠어. 나는 완전히 어린 아기야. 상관없어. 차라리 아기가 되지 뭐. 여보시오! 어이! 거기, 안녕하시오!"

교회 종들이 울리는 소리에 스크루지는 몇 시인지 깨달았다. 댕그랑! 댕그랑! 딩! 동! 딩! 동! 댕그랑! 댕그랑! 오, 근사하구나! 근사해!

창문으로 달려가 스크루지는 창문을 열고 머리를 내밀었다. 농무도 없었고, 안개도 없었다. 날씨는 맑고 밝고 즐겁고 상쾌하고 추웠다. 사람들에게 기운을 주는 유형의 추운 날씨였다. 황금빛 햇살, 거룩한 하늘, 달콤하고 산뜻한 공기, 그리고 즐거운 종소리가 있었다. 오, 근사하구나. 근사해!

"오늘이 며칠이지?" 스크루지가 일요일 예배 보는 옷차림을 하고 내려오는 소년을 불러서 물었다.

"에?" 소년이 놀란 표정으로 말했다.

"오늘이 며칠이니, 착한 아이야?" 스크루지가 말했다.

p.177 "오늘이요?" 소년이 말했다. "크리스마스 날이에요."

"크리스마스 날이라고!" 스크루지가 혼잣말을 했다. "내가 놓치지 않았구나. 유령들이 하룻밤에 그 모든 것을 한 거야. 그들은 원하는 것을 무엇이든 할 수 있다니까. 물론 할 수 있고말고. 어이, 착한 아이야!"

"네!" 소년이 대답했다.

"저 모퉁이에서 다음 거리에 있는 정육점을 아니?" 스크루지가 물었다.

"네, 알아요." 소년이 대답했다.

"총명한 아이로구나!" 스크루지가 말했다. "굉장한 아이야! 그들이 그곳에 걸려 있던 커다란 칠면조고기를 팔았는지 안 팔았는지 아니? 작은 칠면조 말고 큰 놈 말이야?"

"아, 저만큼 큰 놈 말이죠?" 소년이 물었다.

p.178 "참으로 쾌활한 아이로구나!" 스크루지가 말했다. "너와 이야기를 나누게 되어 기쁘구나. 진짜 그렇단다, 얘야!"

"그것은 지금 그곳에 걸려 있어요." 소년이 대답했다.

"그러냐?" 스크루지가 말했다. "가서 사 오너라."

"아저씨는 못 믿어요!" 소년이 소리쳤다.

"아니, 아니야, 나는 정직해지고 있지." 스크루지가 말했다. "가서 그것을 사고, 여기로 그 고기를 가지고 오라고 말해 주렴. 내가 그들에게 그 고기를 어디로 가져갈지 말해 줄 수 있게 말이야. 그리고 주인과 같이 오렴. 그러면 내가 네게 돈을 주마. 주인이랑 같이 5분 내에 돌아오렴. 그러면 너에게 더 많은 돈을 주마!"

소년은 재빨리 떠났다.

"나는 그 칠면조고기를 밥 크래칫의 집으로 보낼 거야!" 손을 비비고 웃으며 스크루지가 속삭였다. "밥은 그것을 누가 보냈는지 모를 거야. 칠면조고기는 막내 팀의 몸집의 두 배야."

스크루지가 주소를 쓰는 손은 떨리고 있었으나, 아무튼 그는 그것을 간신히 썼고 현관문을 열기 위하여 아래층으로 내려갔다. p.179 스크루지는 칠면조고기가 오는 것에 대한 준비를 해 놓았다. 스크루지가 정육점 주인의 도착을 기다리며 그곳에 서 있을 때, 문 두드리는 쇠고리가 그의 눈길을 끌었다.

"내가 살아 있는 한 이 쇠고리를 좋아하게 될 거야!" 쇠고리를 만지며 스크루지가 외쳤다. "나는 전에 이것을 쳐다본 적이 없었지. 참 정직한 표면이구나! 굉장한 쇠고리야. 칠면조고기가 왔군. 거기! 어이! 안녕하시오? 즐거운 크리스마스가 되기를!"

그것은 굉장한 칠면조고기였다. 칠면조가 살아 있을 때, 그놈은 아마도 너무 뚱뚱해서 서 있지도 못했을 것이었다.

"이런, 저놈을 캠든타운까지 가지고 가는 것은 불가능하겠군." 스크루지가 말했다. "자네 마차를 타야겠어."

스크루지는 이 말을 하면서 웃었고, 칠면조 값을 지불하면서 웃었으며, 마차 삯을 지불하면서 웃었다. 스크루지는 소년에게 돈을 주면서 웃었다. 그러나 스크루지는 숨이 차서 다시 자기 의자에 앉았을 때 가장 크게 웃었고 울음이 나올 때까지 웃었다.

p.180 면도하는 것은 쉽지 않았는데, 스크루지의 손이 아주 많이 계속해서 떨렸기 때문이었다. 하지만 설령 자신의 코끝을 베었다고 해도, 스크루지는 여전히 아주 만족했을 것이었다.

스크루지는 가장 좋은 옷을 차려입고 마침내 거리로 나섰다. 스크루지가 현재의 크리스마스 유령과 함께 보았던 것처럼 사람들은 이 무렵 그들의 집에서 나오고 있었다. 뒷짐을 지고 걸어가면서, 스크루지는 유쾌한 미소를 지으며 모두를 바라보았다.

스크루지가 너무나 즐거워 보여서 두세 명의 친절한 사람들은 "안녕하세요, 선생님! 즐거운 크리스마스 보내세요!"라고 말하기도 했다. 그리고 스크루지는 나중에 종종 그것이 자기가 들었던 가장 행복한 소리였다고 말했다.

스크루지는 멀리 가기도 전에 뚱뚱한 신사가 자기를 향해 다가오는 것을 보았다. 그는 전날 스크루지의 사무실 안으로 들어와서 "스크루지와 말리 상점이 맞지요?"라고 말했던 사람이었다. p.181 이 남자가 자신에 관해 틀림없이 생각하고 있을 바를 상상하니 스크루지는 고통이 느껴졌다.

"안녕하시오, 선생." 스크루지가 더 빨리 걸어가서 뚱뚱한 그 신사의 두 손을 잡으며 말했다. "안녕하시오? 어제는 일이 잘 풀리셨기를 바랍니다. 당신은 아주 친절한 분이셨죠. 즐거운 크리스마스 되십시오, 선생!"

"스크루지 씨?" 뚱뚱한 남자가 말했다.

"네." 스크루지가 말했다. "그것이 제 이름이고, 당신에게는 그 이름이 유쾌하지 않을 것 같군요. 죄송합니다. 그리고 부탁을 좀 들어 주시겠습니까?" 스크루지가 그 남자의 귀에 귀엣말을 하기 시작했다.

"이런 세상에!" 그 신사가 놀라서 외쳤다. "친애하는 스크루지 씨, 진심이십니까?"

p.182 "괜찮으시다면요." 스크루지가 말했다. "제가 조금이라도 덜 드리는 일은 없을 것입니다. 제 부탁을 들어주시겠습니까?"

"아이고, 선생님." 신사가 스크루지와 악수를 하며 말했다. "그런 일에 대해 무슨 말씀을 드려야 할지……."

"제발 아무 말씀도 마십시오." 스크루지가 대답했다. "저를 만나러 와 주세요. 한 번 저를 방문하러 와 주시겠습니까?"

"그러겠습니다!" 신사가 외쳤다. 그 신사 역시 그렇게 하고 싶은 것이 분명했다.

"고맙습니다." 스크루지가 말했다. "대단히 감사드립니다. 주님의 축복이 있으시기를!"

스크루지는 교회에 갔고, 거리를 돌아다녔고, 사람들이 달려가는 것을 보았고, 아이들의 머리를 쓰다듬었다. 스크루지는 거지들에게 질문을 하고, 집들의 부엌 안을 내려다보기도 하고, 창문 위로 올려다보기도 하고, 모든 것이 자신을 즐겁게 해 줄 수 있다는 것을 발견했다. 스크루지는 어떠한 산책도, 어떠한 것도 자신에게 그토록 많은 행복을 줄 수 있으리라고 꿈꾸어 본 적이 없었다. 오후에, 스크루지는 조카의 집을 향해 걸어갔다.

p.183 스크루지는 열두 번은 문 앞을 지나치고 나서야 올라가서 문을 두드리기 위한 용기를 냈다. 그러나 스크루지는 마침내 그렇게 했다.

"네 주인이 집에 계시니, 얘야?" 스크루지가 소녀에게 물었다.

"네, 선생님." 소녀가 말했다.

"어디에 계시니, 얘야?" 스크루지가 물었다.

"부인과 함께 식당에 계십니다, 선생님." 소녀가 말했다. "괜찮으시다면, 제가 위층으로 안내해 드릴게요."

"고맙구나." 이미 자기 손을 식당 자물쇠에 얹고 스크루지가 말했다. "주인은 나를 안단다. 내가 이 안으로 들어가마, 얘야."

스크루지는 그것을 천천히 돌려 문을 열었다. 그들은 손님을 위해 만반의 준비를 갖추려고 애쓰며 식탁을 바라보고 있었다.

"프레드!" 스크루지가 말했다.

스크루지의 조카며느리가 놀라서 펄쩍 뛰었다! p.184 스크루지는 조카며느리가 문 근처의 의자에 앉아 있었다는 것을 잊었다.

"이런 세상에!" 프레드가 외쳤다. "저분이 누구야?"

"나다. 네 삼촌 스크루지야." 스크루지가 말했다. "저녁을 먹으러 왔다. 들어가도 되겠니, 프레드?"

스크루지는 5분 동안 그 집에 있었다. 스크루지는 더할 나위 없이 행복했다. 스크루지의 조카며느리는 평소와 똑같아 보였다. 토퍼가 들어왔을 때에도 그랬다. 조카며느리의 여동생이 들어왔을 때에도 그랬다. 모두가 들어왔을 때에도 그랬다. 근사한 파티, 근사한 놀이, 그리고 굉장한 행복이 존재했다!

하지만 스크루지는 다음날 아침 사무실에 일찍 나왔다. 그곳에 먼저 나가서 밥 크래칫이 늦게 오는 것을 잡을 수 있으면 좋을 텐데! 그것이 스크루지가 원하는 것이었다.

그리고 스크루지는 그렇게 했다! 시계가 9시를 쳤다. 밥은 그곳에 없었다. 9시 15분이었다. 밥은 없었다. 밥은 18분 30초나 지각했다. p.185 밥이 사무실로 들어오는 것을 보게 될지도 몰라서 스크루지는 문을 활짝 열어 놓고 앉아 있었다. 밥은 사무실 문을 열기도 전에 모자를 벗었고, 그의 담요도 풀었다. 밥은 재빨리 의자 위에 앉아 일하기 시작했다.

"이봐!" 스크루지가 평소의 목소리로 으르렁거렸다. "왜 늦었나?"

"대단히 죄송합니다, 사장님." 밥이 말했다. "제가 지각을 했습니다."

"그랬어?" 스크루지가 말했다. "그래. 나도 자네가 늦었다고 생각해. 선생님, 괜찮으시다면 이쪽으로 와 보세요."

"일 년에 딱 한 번입니다, 사장님." 사무실에서 모습을 보이며 밥이 빌었다. "다시는 안 그럴 것입니다. 어제는 바쁜 날을 보냈거든요."

"이봐, 내가 한마디 하자면, 나는 이런 식의 상황이 있는 것은 달갑지 않아." 스크루지가 말했다. "그래서 자네의 봉급을 올려 주려고 하네! 즐거운 크리스마스가 보내게, 밥!" 스크루지가 밥의 등을 톡톡 두드리며 솔직하게 말했다.

p.186 밥이 당황하여 자기 사장을 바라보았다.

"자네의 봉급을 올려줄 것이고, 살려고 애쓰는 자네 가족들을 도와줄 걸세." 스크루지가 말했다. "우리는 오늘 근사한 저녁을 먹으며 자네의 가족들에 관해 이야기할 것이네, 밥! 불을 피우게!"

스크루지는 자기가 약속한 것 이상으로 모든 일을 했다. 죽지 않은 막내 팀에게, 스크루지는 양부였다. 스크루지는 좋은 친구, 좋은 주인, 그리고 좋은 사람이 되었다. 스크루지는 그 도시에서, 아니 세상에서 가장 좋은 사람들 중 한 명이 되었다. 어떤 사람들은 스크루지 내면의 변화를 비웃었지만, 스크루지는 그들이 비웃게 내버려두었고, 그들의 말에 귀를 기울이지 않았다.

사람들이 비웃지 않는 좋은 일이 이 세상에서는 아무것도 일어날 수 없다는 것을 잘 알 만큼 스크루지는 현명했다. 스크루지는 이러한 사람들이 무지하고 눈이 멀었다는 것을 깨달았다. 스크루지 자신의 마음은 웃었고, 그것으로 그는 충분했다.

p.187 스크루지가 다른 유령을 다시 만나는 법은 없었다. 사람들은 늘 스크루지가 그 누구보다도 크리스마스를 더 잘 축하하는 방법을 안다고 말했다. 우리 모두 크리스마스를 잘 축하하는 것을 배우기를! 그리고 또한 막내 팀이 말했듯이, 모두에게 주님의 축복이 함께 하기를!